So You Want to Be a Superintendent?

William Hayes

The Scarecrow Press, Inc.
A Scarecrow Education Book
Lanham, Maryland, and London
2001

SCARECROW PRESS, INC.
A Scarecrow Education Book

Published in the United States of America
by Scarecrow Press, Inc.
4720 Boston Way
Lanham, Maryland 20706
http://www.scarecrowpress.com

4 Pleydell Gardens, Folkestone
Kent CT20 2DN, England

British Library Cataloguing in Publication Information Available

Library of Congress Cataloging-in-Publication Data

Hayes, William, 1938–
　　So you want to be a superintendent? / William Hayes.
　　　p. cm.
　　Includes bibliographical references and index.
　　ISBN 0-8108-3928-8 (alk. paper) — ISBN 0-8108-3929-6 (paper : alk. paper)
　　　1. School superintendents—United States. 2. School management and
　　organization—Vocational guidance—United States. I. Title.

LB2831.72.H36 2001
371.2'011—dc21   00-061943

♾ ™ The paper used in this publication meets the minimum requirements of
American National Standard for Information Sciences—Permanence of
Paper for Printed Library Materials, ANSI/NISO Z39.48-1992.
Manufactured in the United States of America.

CONTENTS

PREFACE

In my freshman Foundations of Education class, we always consider the role of the superintendent of schools. As part of this discussion, I ask the students whether they would consider someday becoming a superintendent. Inevitably no more than two or three hands are raised, and often these are students who are unlikely candidates for leadership positions. When I query the class as to why they have no interest in becoming superintendents, the answers are always the same. Their responses revolve around two themes. First, they say that they do not want to deal with being "hassled" by parents, teachers, community members, and the media. Others talk about the fact that they are not going into education to be politicians but rather to work with children. Nearly all of these students who reject the idea of becoming superintendents feel they want to make a difference in the lives of children and that this can be best done as a classroom teacher.

These comments cause me to respond with a brief lecture on the fact that superintendents can and do make a difference and that it is essential that at least some of our "best and brightest people" become educational administrators. I always suspect that my impassioned pleas have very limited impact on these young people. Still, I remain convinced that unless our society can somehow provide a generation of effective educational leaders, our current school reform initiatives will have little impact on the education of young people.

This book is being written for anyone who has an interest in the superintendency, but my primary goal is to reach individuals who might consider someday a career as a superintendent. It is clear that not everyone in education should aspire to the position, but it is also evident that there is a growing need for outstanding superintendents. Consultants who are seeking applicants are reporting that the pool of qualified candidates is alarmingly small. There is also no question that the demands of the position have never been greater.

With these factors in mind, it is my purpose to help explain both the challenges and the rewards of the position. All superintendents will feel significant pressures as they attempt to move their school districts forward. Certainly, they will also experience frustration during prolonged contract negotiations and the disappointment when bond issues are defeated. On the other hand, you will enjoy the very positive realization that your decisions and actions have helped children.

A final objective of this book is to share with the reader some thoughts on how to succeed as a superintendent. Although many people will be glad to give you advice and numerous books such as this one are available, you will bear the ultimate responsibility for the effectiveness and efficiency of your school district. Every superintendency is different, but certain practices and approaches have been shown to help others.

The suggestions contained in this book are based on my twenty-one years' experience as a superintendent. Those years were happy and rewarding ones for me and my family. The superintendency offers opportunities and challenges that are not available in many careers. Because your words and actions will be taken seriously by others, the position allows a superintendent to give recognition when it is deserved and help to those in distress. Each day of your professional life will be different. I have seldom heard of a superintendent who was bored with the job. Your problems will be intellectually challenging, but when solutions are found, satisfaction ensues. Individuals you have recommended for employment will become master teachers and administrators. Successful graduates from your school district will be a constant source of pride.

Many talented and committed people have served as superintendents of schools. These individuals have made a positive difference in their school districts and have, as a result, earned the respect and gratitude of their entire community. More important, they have created a legacy as leaders who have left their school district a better place for teachers to teach and children to learn. For me and many of my fellow retirees, the superintendency represented a calling in which we are honored to serve. It is my hope that the position, however difficult it has become, will continue to attract people who are truly committed to improving schools. I write this book in hope that it might in some way be helpful in encouraging qualified people to step forward and accept the challenge.

ACKNOWLEDGMENTS

Many people have helped with this book. I am indebted to Carol Babcock and Katrina Oyer, who are members of the office staff in the Teacher Education Division of Roberts Wesleyan College. Andrew Eckert, a student worker in the office, typed a portion of the manuscript. Another student and now a teacher, Kristen Bianchi, has been a crucial partner in this project, as well as the other books published by Scarecrow Press. Kristen's attention to detail, careful editing, and excellent typing have been essential to completing this volume. Finally, I thank my wife, Nancy, whose patience and willingness to proofread and give suggestions have made this book possible.

CHAPTER ONE

The Superintendency Today

Considering a career as a superintendent of schools? Here is some advice. First, it is not an easy job. Perhaps it has always been difficult, but knowledgeable observers seem to agree that as we begin a new century, the challenge of the position is greater than ever. Much has changed during the past half century.

In 1950, an author writing a novel that would include a stereotypical superintendent of schools might describe the individual in this way. The superintendent would be a white male who dressed in a dark suit with a conservative tie, who might look like a United States senator. Citizens, faculty, and staff in this fictional portrait would see the superintendent as a symbol of authority. He would have the respect of many and perhaps be feared by some. In this era before teachers unions, he would be the unchallenged leader of the school district. Very likely, this mythical superintendent would be in his fifties and might have worked in the district for many years. With the board of education, the superintendent would make the important decisions, and school district employees would accept them without protest. The board would include primarily prominent citizens who, out of the sense of duty, sought board membership as an appropriate way to serve their community. Most would be well-known individuals who were successful in business or their professions. Few board members would be interested in involving themselves in the day-to-day management of the district. That was the superintendent's job.

The typical superintendent today is functioning in a different type of setting. It has become quite clear that the position in the twenty-first century is very different from that of the twentieth century. One of the reasons for the difference seems to be that boards of education have changed. Because conflict and confrontation have become more common at meetings, many potential candidates see board membership as a thankless job that will only involve them in unwanted controversy.

Some community members who have followed in the media the confrontations between teacher unions and school districts have concluded
that they would rather do public service in a less stressful environment.
Board candidates often think "I don't want to get on the school board
and make the teachers mad at me. I have children in that school district."

If individuals seeking merely to do public service are less likely to consider school board membership, who are the people who are deciding to
step forward? Unfortunately, it appears that boards are attracting a good
number of "single-issue" candidates. These individuals could represent a
taxpayer's league whose primary interest is to lower property taxes. Others might wish to establish programs for the gifted or to do more for children diagnosed with attention deficit disorder. There are, of course, those
whose primary interest is "getting rid of" a superintendent, principal, or
basketball coach.

Board members are also not continuing in the position as long as they
used to. These frequent changes in board membership create unique problems for a superintendent. It is not uncommon for the majority of a board
that hired a superintendent to turn over in three or four years. When the
new members have a different agenda from those who selected the superintendent, it is not difficult to foresee potential conflict.

Along with the frequent changes in board membership, superintendents
must contend with increased public and media interest in their schools. In
a nation in which opinion polls consistently rank improving education as
the number one priority of the American people, it is not surprising that
both the media and citizens are paying more attention to what is going on
in the schools. Twenty-five years ago, many school districts had board
meetings with few or no visitors. Sessions were anything but exciting, and
the superintendent was most often in charge. Because boards saw the superintendent as the "expert," they often accepted without question their
chief school officer's recommendations. Citizens in the community were
unlikely to come to board meetings unless a serious issue was on the
agenda.

Board meetings began to change in the early eighties when a national
recession caused school budgets to become tighter. For this and for other
reasons, interest in board meetings in districts increased. Spectators became commonplace, and many boards introduced a time during the meeting for comments by the public. In some districts the regular board of education meeting became the "best show in town." Newspaper reporters
began to attend regularly rather than calling the superintendent the morning after the meeting. It became more common for districts to have their

board sessions broadcast live on the radio and sometimes even by local television stations. Some board members took advantage of this new public interest to play to the audience and to the media. Previously, many superintendents could almost script board meetings. As a result of this increased attention, it has become more difficult to predict what might happen at a meeting and how the session would be reported the next day in the newspaper.

Along with the challenge of working with the board of education, the emergence of strong employee unions has had a significant impact on the superintendent's job. Prior to the formation of unions, teachers were most often left out of the decision-making process. This was even true with matters that directly affected the teachers' work in the classroom. Conditions of employment such as salaries, fringe benefits, and the hours of the workday were usually determined by the superintendent and the board. As unions challenged this approach beginning in the late sixties, the effect on the superintendent's role was dramatic. In most districts today, it would be impossible for the superintendent to establish unilaterally with the board the rate of the salary increase for all employees. It is also no longer possible for a superintendent to direct that the school year should be increased by three days or that teachers will, as part of their regular job, chaperone school events.

Sharing power with unions of teachers, bus drivers, and secretaries has severely limited the once unquestioned authority of the superintendent. The role now frequently places the chief school officer in a very uncomfortable position between the board of education and the employees of the district.

Although unions and changes in boards of education have added to the challenges that face superintendents, the traditional functions of the position have not changed markedly. For example, the superintendent remains the chief public spokesperson for the board and the school district. Still, this task must now sometimes be shared between a strong board president and the teacher union president.

As chief school officer, many ceremonial functions still need to be performed. The superintendent will speak to the faculty and staff each year prior to the opening of school. There will be numerous welcoming speeches at school events and meetings as well as participation in the graduation ceremony, retirement parties, and new faculty and staff orientations. These responsibilities will always be part of the job, although when problems arise in the district, the number of invitations a superintendent receives can be affected.

Often the chief school officer will represent the district at various meetings in the community. Most successful administrators welcome these opportunities as a way to share publicly with the community the positive work the school district is doing and also to enlist support for school programs. When controversial issues are facing the district, these occasions can be difficult. When state aid reductions are occurring in a district and taxes are being increased, superintendents will not always look forward to speaking engagements at the senior citizens center.

The budget and the academic programs are, of course, primary responsibilities of the superintendent of schools. In both of these important areas, there are strong arguments for using advisory committees made up of teachers, parents, community members, and sometimes students. With the trend toward additional "site-based management," the superintendent will often need to weigh the recommendations of individual school committees in making program and budget decisions. It is necessary to plan and guide a decision-making process that is often cumbersome and subject to breakdowns.

As schools become more democratic, the superintendent's role has required new skills in managing advisory groups. As the institutional leader, the chief school officer must still have a clear vision for the school district and be able to articulate these ideas. Today superior communications skills are as essential as ever, but they are not enough to guarantee success. One must be a strategist who can ensure correct decisions despite a maze of committees and interest groups. This requires careful planning and great diplomacy. Merely issuing directives from the central office can often alienate people and lose support for a superintendent. If there is a need to improve the district's reading program, the superintendent must find a way to "facilitate" the necessary changes. Many chief school officers now feel that the best way to bring about improvement of any kind is to create an environment in which individuals within the school and community will seek to initiate and implement change. In other words, many feel that "bottom-up" innovations are more effective than mandated "top-down" changes.

It is questionable how a superintendent from the 1950s would have managed in this new environment. He would have had to modify his management style and methods and would have had to become sensitive to a number of new forces within the district. For instance, it is no longer appropriate to think of principals and teachers as merely employees. They must be treated as fellow professionals who expect to participate in the decision-making process. Although teachers have not yet reached the same position within their institutions as college professors, they have come a long way in most districts in gaining the right to be heard.

In some ways, public school administration has become unique. Superintendents lack the power of chief executive officers in most businesses to hire and fire employees easily and to impose new programs and policies on their organization. As a result, the superintendent must have a clear plan for carrying out change in this increasingly democratic environment. It is essential to know how and when to use committees. Ensuring that the appropriate interest groups have a voice usually helps avoid problems later in the process. Being able to mediate and compromise are essential skills for today's superintendent. This must be done without losing the trust of divergent individuals and groups. While working with others, the superintendent must continually strive to do what is best for children. A chief school officer who is perceived as an unprincipled politician always trying to manipulate people will quickly lose respect.

Playing these various roles and exercising the necessary skills to perform them successfully will test any leader. Because many superintendents are not able to maintain adequate support in their district, the turnover rate among superintendents is currently at an unhealthy high.

One of the great dangers inherent in the superintendent's job is the loss of the confidence of the faculty and staff. Although the public does not always perceive it as a major problem, a no confidence vote by the faculty can make it very uncomfortable for a superintendent. At the same time, if a chief school officer is seen by a majority of the public as being incompetent, popularity with the employees will not be enough to protect the superintendent. By far, the quickest way for a person to lose his or her job is when there is not sufficient support of the majority of the board of education. Frequently conflict erupts between the board and the superintendent over how the district should be managed. Superintendents can be very jealous of their powers and often are unhappy when they feel that board members are attempting to micromanage the district. On the other hand, some board members are sensitive to the possibility that they are being considered as merely "rubber stamps" for the administration. Because superintendents lack the protection of tenure, any conflict that turns a majority of a board against their chief school officer can lead to an end of the superintendent's employment in the district.

A new factor is also contributing to the rapid turnover rate of superintendents. As schools become increasingly accountable to the public, the survival of superintendents depends more and more on their ability to raise the academic achievement of students. Publication of report cards for schools that compare test scores with other schools is now common. The test data appears in local newspapers; as a result, citizens have an opportunity to compare their students' test scores with other schools. A superintendent whose students continue to do poorly becomes like a baseball manager who has a losing record. Although many complex factors contribute to low test scores, if there is not improvement, the superintendent will eventually be held accountable. Superintendents in the past never had to worry about this type of pressure.

Accountability is just one aspect of the educational reform movement that schools continue to experience as we enter a new century. Superintendents are expected to have their district in the forefront of reform and change. A superintendent who did not lead in the school computer revolution of the nineties would have been considered negligent. There is no question that the public wants to see computers in the schools. It does not seem to matter that faculty training should come first or that there is scant evidence that computers in every classroom will automatically enhance school performance.

Parents and sometimes teachers have also pushed districts to move rapidly to the inclusion of special education students in the regular classroom and to block scheduling in the secondary school. Superintendents who are cautious about these innovations are considered by some to be reactionaries and enemies of progress. The nationwide effort to improve schools has created the expectation that superintendents must be agents of change. The yearly evaluation of a superintendent's work often emphasizes the success of the chief school officer in meeting goals related to academic achievement. Even where no specific objective targets exist, the superintendent must demonstrate that forward movement and innovation have occurred during the previous year.

If there have been many additional challenges for superintendents of schools during the past fifty years, one can assume that change will only accelerate in the future. As we scan the current situation, a number of projections seem feasible. Presently a nationwide voucher system seems unlikely, but the idea of school choice remains very popular. Both magnet schools and charter schools are growing in number. It is interesting to speculate on how the issue of school choice will affect the role of superintendents.

Along with school choice, increased diversity within the student population seems inevitable. Undoubtedly more pressure, especially in urban areas, will emerge to hire nonwhite teachers and administrators. Currently, the percentage of minority and women superintendents is very low. For women, at least, this trend is changing quickly and likely to continue. Increased student diversity will also fuel support for multicultural education.

Another obvious trend in the future will be the involvement of parents and community members in school affairs. Most would agree with the African proverb used by first lady Hillary Clinton as the title of her book: "It takes the whole village to raise a child." Schools have already begun to reach out to their communities.

Although some may regard it as only a passing phenomenon, it is hard to believe that concern about violence and security in our schools will disappear. The same is true of the problem of young people abusing drugs and alcohol. We have not come close to dealing with these issues successfully.

All of these problems will continue to challenge us in the twenty-first century, but one cannot help but wonder about the current heavy emphasis on standards, testing, and accountability. Given the history of American education, one can easily conclude that we will soon experience a strong countermovement that will forcefully argue that our current obsession with standards is hurting too many children. Such a reaction is already occurring in some communities. The *New York Times* on December 3, 1999, cited the following examples:

- Wisconsin agreed to parent demands to withdraw a test required of every student for high school graduation.
- After only one in ten Arizona sophomores passed a new state math test, the Arizona Board of Education agreed to parents' demands to reconsider the test.
- The Virginia Board of Education agreed in principle to revise a new policy requiring schools to show that seventy percent of students were meeting state testing requirements by 2007. Only seven percent of Virginia schools met that standard in spring 1999.
- Massachusetts set the passing grade lower on its rigorous new tests.
- Los Angeles school administrators are considering scaling back their plan to end automatic promotions in all grades after they calculated that nearly one of every two students would have to be held back.[1]

The result of this type of community reaction could well lead us away from the thinking of E. D. Hirsh and back to John Dewey. We could soon be talking about trying to make our schools more "student-friendly." Such a countermovement would be very much in keeping with the pendulum swings we have so often seen in education. If such a swing in public opinion gains added force, superintendents will have to hold on tight. Even if the predominant philosophy does shift, the public and the state and national governments will continue to seek excellence in our schools. Accountability for our educational programs will continue to be with us.

One cannot consider the future of public education and ignore the impact of technology. It is impossible to imagine the demise of schools and libraries as we know them, but neither is it likely that computers are just another educational fad. The next generation of superintendents will have to be much more knowledgeable about computers than those chief school officers who participated during the last decade in the introduction of computers into our schools.

Along with new technology, another major challenge appears to be facing many schools. With increased enrollment in many areas of the country and a large number of teacher retirements, superintendents will face a growing need to find ways to recruit and retain quality teachers. This problem is already present in many areas of the United States. For most urban and some rural schools, it has become a critical issue. Unlike in recent years, many superintendents will be working very hard to "sell" their district to potential teacher candidates. Once teachers have taken a job, boards of education and administrators will have to become much more cognizant of the need to create a climate in their schools that will keep good teachers from leaving their district. This is just another of the increased challenges that will face superintendents as we begin the twenty-first century.

While the future holds many unanswered questions, a number of hopeful signs are evident as we enter a new millennium. The national leadership of both the National Education Association and the American Federation of Teachers has moderated significantly their previous confrontational approach. As teacher salaries have risen in a number of areas, many districts seem to be experiencing a more rapid and reasonable negotiation process. This trend can only help superintendents as they attempt to bring about positive change.

A second factor also should prove an aid to helping a school leader bring about academic improvement. Educational research seems to be improving in quality and quantity. Currently, research studies show that reducing class size in kindergarten through the third grade can produce lasting academic growth if the students are being taught by well-qualified teachers. Researchers also seem to agree that money spent on quality preschool programs can make a difference in student achievement throughout a student's academic career. Time and money spent on appropriate faculty and staff development is also justified by current research. These findings can assist a superintendent to establish priorities and to justify reforms within school districts.

Despite these valuable research findings, the educational community remains divided on questions such as academic grouping. Even with the current trend toward mixed groups, most observers believe this will continue to be a contentious debate well into the twenty-first century.

Some may conclude that the issues raised in this chapter have made the job of a school superintendent untenable. The expectation that anyone can stay in one community for decades and become a respected figure seems increasingly more difficult. Despite all of the potential problems, it is possible to be optimistic about the future of the superintendency in the United States. Most observers would agree that those entering the profession today are just as committed to the profession as were teachers in previous generations. Along with their commitment, they also know more about teaching and learning than teachers entering the profession in the past. Teacher preparation institutions are improving, as their programs are emphasizing stronger liberal arts components and more meaningful education courses. Statewide teacher certification examinations are eliminating many candidates who are poorly prepared for the profession. Better salaries and an increased demand for new teachers have allowed teacher education programs to attract many excellent people of all ages. Increasingly outstanding individuals are moving from responsible careers outside education to become teachers. The graduate teacher education program at my college has included students who have earned a Ph.D. in their subject area, former high-ranking military officers, and management personnel for a variety of businesses. Many of these individuals are excellent potential candidates for administrative positions.

With this increasingly rich pool of candidates, our challenge in education is to encourage the right people to seek leadership positions and to prepare them effectively for what they will face. From all indications, we are currently doing very poorly in recruiting and preparing future educational leaders. The reasons for this failure seem to be inherent in both the state administrative certification programs and in the college programs that are preparing educational administrators. In fall 1999, the American Association of School Administrators (AASA) published a study entitled

Licensure/Certification of the Next Generation of School Superintendents: Conclusions from a National Study. The following conclusions were reached as a result of this research project:

Conclusion 1: In establishing certification requirements, the policy-making bodies in most states either ignored or rejected the arguments and recommendations from the literature on the preparation of educational leaders.

Conclusion 2: By not including changes recommended in the literature as part of new certification requirements for superintendents in recent revisions, the states, individually and collectively, missed a historic opportunity to make dramatic changes in preparation programs.

Conclusion 3: For most states and universities, there is no specific superintendent preparation program, only an extended principle preparation program.

Conclusion 4: More than half the states have no assessment requirements for superintendent candidates. For these states, the absence of such requirements indicates an unwillingness to use assessment as a screening device to limit the pool for the superintendency.

Conclusion 5: For almost half the states, policymakers view prior administrative experiences as neither necessary nor valuable to the new superintendent.

Conclusion 6: In most states, students completing the program of superintendent preparation may likely be unprepared and unable to select appropriate reform strategies for their schools.

Conclusion 7: Few states recognize or take seriously the demand to prepare future educational leaders for meeting the needs of the diverse group of students entering public schools today.[2]

If we assume that these conclusions are not total exaggerations, then our society must do a better job in selecting and preparing our future educational leaders. This very important issue is the subject of the next chapter.

NOTES

1. The *New York Times*, 3 December 1999.
2. *Licensure/Certification of the Next Generation of School Superintendents,* AASA Online, (1999).

CHAPTER TWO

Preparing for the Superintendency

Although what is being done to prepare superintendents may seem inadequate, it is still far superior to the academic training received by many chief school officers in the past. For previous generations of superintendents, it was not unusual to be promoted to the position with little or no academic preparation. During the 1970s, it was possible to be appointed as a building principal in New York state with as few as two administration courses. It was not uncommon for a teacher to be made a principal even with no courses and be allowed to work in the role of acting principal until the minimum requirement was met. Even as a superintendent, for which the requirement was twenty-four hours of administrative coursework, it was common for a person to be appointed and given the opportunity to meet the academic requirements at a later time. Many colleges had no formal curriculum for administrative preparation but merely offered a "cafeteria-style" group of classes. In the early 1970s, the idea of an extended administrative internship was almost nonexistent. The result for many was that most of what was learned about being a superintendent came from on-the-job training.

Today, many states are requiring much more preparation for their school administrators. Still, since the 1980s, a number of major efforts have been made to improve college programs leading to certification of future superintendents. The American Association of School Administrators (AASA), the National Association of Elementary School Principals (NAESP), and the National Association of Secondary School Principals (NASSP), along with a coalition of national groups concerned about education, came together to improve programs for school administrators. This group later was responsible for the formation of the Interstate School Licensure Coalition (ISSLC), which has created a test to evaluate administrative degrees and certify candidates. Although the examination has only been adopted by a few states, others are considering it.

Improvement of school administration programs is also a goal of the National Council for the Accreditation of Teacher Education (NCATE). As part of the national accreditation process, NCATE has studied the administration component of a number of schools of education. Often during these evaluations, visiting teams have found programs with very few full-time faculty, no internship programs, and a lack of coursework in the areas of technology and changing student populations. Thus far, most colleges of education have avoided NCATE accreditation for their programs in educational administration. This lack of interest in pursuing accreditation includes famous universities as well as most smaller institutions.[1]

Presently, neither the attempt to require national accreditation for educational administration programs nor a national test for prospective principals and superintendents has had major impact on reforming preparation programs. The frustration of the major national organizations representing administrators has become so great that they are actively discussing establishing their own programs "in partnership with a profit making company or an entrepreneurial university."[2]

A president of the AASA has gone so far as to suggest that the only way to improve the current college programs is to totally eliminate the master's degree in educational administration. He argues that these programs attract a good number of students merely looking for the easiest way to earn a master's degree. A significant number of these students never even seek a position in administration. Because there is pressure on these programs to maintain their high enrollment figures, departments of education are hesitant to increase the rigor of their curriculums. With their low entrance requirements and less than demanding classes, the educational administration programs remain very profitable for their college or university. The president believes that leaders in these institutions will never voluntarily undertake reform without strong competition from quality programs. The result could be that together, ASSA, NASSP, and NAESP will provide that competition. Along with offering their own educational programs, these groups are considering introducing a plan for national certification of school administrators. The standards and examination established by ISSLC would be the basis for this certification process. In addition to this initiative is the recent effort of the Educational Testing Service and five states (Illinois, Kentucky, Missouri, Mississippi, and North Carolina) to establish a "performance-based" test for licensure.[3]

Despite these efforts, the quality of academic programs preparing school administrators varies greatly. For the most part, colleges have tailored their curriculums to provide the minimum requirements for state certification. The major exception is at those universities where a doctoral program in educational administration is offered. These programs not only are more rigorous but also place a high priority on research. Of course, there are also the added hurdles of oral and written examinations along with the required dissertation. Still, it should be noted that the vast majority of superintendents in the United States do not complete a doctoral program. Instead, most have their academic training at colleges that are providing programs leading to certification or licensure. For this reason, it would seem that the place to institute positive change must initially be in these state programs. A quick examination of what is now being required by the states can help us understand the current situation.

A study of the state certification requirements as they were reported in a 1999 publication noted that twenty-seven states require teaching or administrative experience. The amount of experience required for certification ranged from one year as a minimum in Oklahoma to eight years of experience in Rhode Island. The most common requirement for administrative certification was a master's degree, along with additional graduate study. Approximately three-fourths of the states require this academic preparation. Another smaller group of states requires future superintendents to have an internship and/or previous administrative experience. Here again, the amount of time required ranges from one year in several states to five years in Louisiana. Only about a dozen states have teaching certification as a requirement for becoming a superintendent. A smaller number of states stipulate that a superintendent must be formally recommended by an approved college or university. California and Connecticut have added to their requirements that superintendents have training in the field of special education. Finally, about ten states have no specific certification requirements for superintendents. Even this rather cursory examination of state certification programs indicates the variety of requirements established by individual states.

Although it is tempting to try to design a certification program and college curriculum for future superintendents, I have decided to attempt the more modest task of outlining those subjects and skills that I believe would best prepare an individual to become a superintendent. First and foremost, it would seem helpful for an educational leader to be conversant with history. It is especially important to understand the story of the development of education in the United States. Without historical perspective, a leader is unable to view current events as a part of a continuing saga in which we are all players. Much of what we are experiencing in our schools today is the result of or in reaction to previous events and movements. It is important as we begin a new century to know how in the last one hundred years we have moved through progressive education to the standards movement. Also, a superintendent must have a clear understanding of racial and gender history to deal with these current issues.

Along with history, reading biographies and some fiction can help school administrators learn more about the challenges they will face. Books such as David McCullough's *Truman* or David Donald's one-volume biography of Lincoln are examples of life stories of leaders that can be helpful to superintendents. Two very effective novels that deal with political leadership are Edwin O'Connor's *The Last Hurrah* and *All The King's Men* by Robert Penn Warren. In regard to the political decision-making process, two excellent books are *The Master* and *Corridors of Power* by twentieth-century British author C. P. Snow.

H. G. Wells has written in *The Outline of History* that the study of "human history is in essence a history of ideas." The ideas that Wells refers to can be found in the works of some of our great philosophers. As educators we should be aware of the writings of Socrates, Plato, and a number of modern thinkers. Much of what John Dewey wrote more than half a century ago is still relevant to the educational decisions we are facing today.

Many of these decisions involve ethical and moral choices. Medical, law, and business colleges have seen a dramatic increase of courses in professional ethics. It could also be helpful to introduce our future educational leaders to some of the different choices they will be forced to make in their profession. An excellent way to prepare administrators to make ethical and sound choices is through the use of case studies in the classroom.

The use of case studies has long been an instructional method used in the education of doctors, lawyers, and business leaders. Such cases can not only be helpful with ethical problems but also can give future superintendents an introduction to making personnel, program, and budget decisions. In addition, it should be noted that classes devoted to the discussion of realistic problems can enliven administrative courses, which are too often dominated by faculty lectures. Students who are taking an evening class after a long day of teaching often find it difficult to sit and listen to a teacher talk for three hours.

Today, there is little question that much can be gained by exposing future administrators to the body of information we now call management theory. Learning about the importance of mission statements and organizational objectives can be as essential for a superintendent as for an aspiring business chief executive officer. Educational leaders should know the work of Pete Drucker and be able to discuss the principles of total quality management. As the chief school officer of an educational institution, it is important to know how to develop strategic and tactical plans.

In his book *Victory in Our Schools,* the late John Stanford, the very successful superintendent in Seattle, Washington, emphasized how he used the planning techniques he learned as an army officer and county executive to give focus to his academic improvement program. In the introduction of his book, Stanford states that

> people wondered when I was hired how someone with no background in education could possibly fix schools. But Seattle didn't need an educator—Seattle needed a professional manager to determine whether or not all functions of the school district were working to promote the goals of the district, to eliminate those that weren't, and refocus the others to academic achievement. And Seattle needed a leader to galvanize the entire city into action.[4]

The appeal to boards of education such as Seattle of candidates from outside the educational establishment can possibly be explained by a number of factors. Especially in many urban districts where schools have just not improved, a board might well conclude after a series of unsuccessful chief school officers that it is time to try something different. As most board members are people from the private enterprise sector, it is not surprising that they might look to a leader from outside to bring about change in their districts. This is especially true when board members have become frustrated with the failure of the system to respond to more traditional leadership styles. This willingness to experiment would also be encouraged if board members perceived public education primarily as a business operation.

Knowledge of management principles was undoubtedly helpful to John Stanford. It is also likely that his experience outside education aided him in succeeding as a superintendent. Because most schools of educational administration have few if any professors with experience outside education, it might well be helpful to invite into classes guest speakers who are managers in other fields. Perhaps such a person could even team-teach a course on management principles with an education professor. In any case, educational leaders can benefit from learning about the art and science of management.

Many of the management decisions made by a superintendent take place within a political environment. Today, the word *politician* has a very negative connotation for most Americans, and certainly a superintendent of schools would wish to avoid such a label. The fact is that every day of their professional lives, superintendents are involved in political activity. Political activity or the practice of politics is not inherently bad. Both Abraham Lincoln and Franklin Delano Roosevelt were politicians, yet history has been kind to them. *Webster's New Collegiate Dictionary* defines a politician as "one versed in the art of government." If we accept this definition, a successful chief school officer must be a politician.

Governance of schools in the United States is a very complex issue. Our federal system divides decision-making power among national, state, and local governments. Even though it provides only approximately seven percent of the funding for public schools, the federal government is playing an increasingly significant role in education. Federal legislation such as Title I of the Elementary and Secondary Education Act, Title IX of the 1972 Educational Amendments Act, and Public Law 94-142 has had tremendous impact on school programs and budgets. Of course, decisions made in the federal courts on subjects such as integration and school prayer also have been pivotal in the history of education in the United States.

State government remains perhaps the key player in the governance of schools. Bureaucracies at the state level, along with the legislature, create curriculum and statewide testing programs. The fact that states provide approximately fifty percent of the incomes for schools causes the annual question of state aid to be a major concern for superintendents. As leaders of an educational institution, superintendents must be well versed in their states' political processes. Many superintendents maintain a close relationship with their local state legislators and, along with their administrative organizations, attempt to affect decisions in state government.

On the local level, the superintendent is often politically active. Knowledge of how politics work in a local community is absolutely essential for any superintendent. One must be aware of who the true leaders are in the community. If these individuals decide to oppose a bond issue or a budget vote, it is often very difficult for a superintendent to overcome such opposition. While an understanding of politics is important, a superintendent must also have an understanding of school law. Unless the school employs an attorney on the payroll, calling on a lawyer for answers on legal matters can be very costly to the district. Faculty, staff, and community members also expect that their superintendent will be well informed and able to answer their questions.

One of the main issues that a school leader will have to deal with in the political arena is school funding. To do this effectively, a superintendent must know something about the economics of education. Besides understanding the macroeconomics of American capitalism, the chief school officer must learn to understand state aid formulas, the auditor's annual financial report, and how tax rates are determined. Many first-year superintendents must rely almost solely on the district business office to carry out the financial tasks of the school district. Although it is not necessary that the superintendent be an accountant, as the chief executive officer it is important to understand and be heavily involved in the financial matters of the district. In the end, it is the superintendent who is responsible for prudent financial planning and for keeping the district from overspending the budget. This is especially true in relation to the development of annual budgets, capital projects, and state aid applications. These matters are much too important to be totally delegated to others. Even some doctoral programs in educational administration are sometimes weak in the area of finance. Because the economics of education are constantly changing, a superintendent must work hard to stay abreast of developments at every level of government.

Another essential educational requirement for future leaders is an understanding of the changing demographics of today's students. The increasing diversity of many communities has implications for every phase of school programs. Our future superintendents must become sensitive to issues relating to race, ethnicity, and religion. The chief school officer is likely to be dealing with individuals representing groups of all types. Only a broad knowledge of the social issues of our times will help administrators when they come in contact with such groups as gay adolescents, Christian conservatives, and parents or groups representing Native Americans.

[Although knowledge of sociology, history, philosophy, management principles, economics, political science, and technology provides a helpful background for superintendents,]it must always be remembered that the primary goal is to help children learn more effectively. To do this well, one must know something about curriculum and effective teaching methods. First and foremost, a superintendent is a professional educator. The only way a person can be a true professional is to continue to learn more and more about his or her primary field of expertise. As mentioned earlier, we now have more reliable research to help us make better decisions. Because in the past, few superintendents who did not seek a doctoral degree had little exposure to educational research, many educational decisions were made without considering research findings. Too often, new programs were instituted that had never been fully validated. Not only was the superintendent often uninformed on educational research, but the same was true of many other teachers and administrators. Looking back, our school district should have spent more on quality staff development, smaller class sizes for grades K through three, and support for excellent preschool programs. A failure of too many superintendents is to become overly engrossed in the political, economic, and social issues of the district and to spend little or no time on educational programs. A strong background in teaching and learning will better prepare a superintendent to be a positive force in this most important leadership function.

As we enter a new century, it is now also absolutely necessary that a chief school officer be technologically literate. In 1994, many superintendents did not have computers in their offices. Today in most schools, the pace has quickened dramatically, and a superintendent who is unprepared to lead in this area will be considered incompetent. Probably only a few district offices today do not have computers, and the superintendent is likely to spend a considerable amount of time working on his or her own personal computer. Most districts have during the past five years participated in major initiatives to bring computers not only into offices but into their schools' classrooms. A superintendent who is not prepared to lead in this technological revolution would most likely be considered not only behind the times but perhaps incompetent.

A final component of the academic program of someone seeking to be a superintendent is a realistic opportunity for practical experience. When this occurs, students often comment that their internship was the single most valuable aspect of their administrative training. It is extremely difficult for educational administration programs to develop meaningful internships for their students. Unlike undergraduate teacher education students, most people participating in an educational administration curriculum are older and are working full-time during the day. Most often they are full-time teachers who cannot afford to take time off to be full-time interns. As a result, many students do their work as interns after school, during vacations, or in the summer. In any case, they are interns who are working when few, if any, students are even in the building. Because these internships are most often unpaid, they are forced into already busy schedules and fail to provide a realistic administrative experience.

Those administrators who have worked with intern programs in local colleges have undoubtedly seen weaknesses in the curriculum. Often, college intern supervisors have dealt with far too many students and contributed little to the program. In some cases, these supervisors lacked any experience themselves as school administrators. As a result, the effectiveness of the internship was almost totally determined by the host administrator. Too often, school administrators take advantage of interns and assign narrow busy work tasks that contribute little to the students' education.

To prepare administrators effectively, we must find ways to provide realistic internship experiences. The best way to do this is to offer full-time paid experiences with interested and effective mentors. When an intern is able to work full-time in a district and have real responsibilities, the experience can be positive for both the student and the school district. For this to happen, an administrative intern must be given a leave from their regular duties. At a time when the pool of quality administrative candidates continues to shrink, school districts would be wise to finance sabbatical or other leaves for their own future leaders. In February 2000, the city school district in Rochester, New York, agreed to pay thirty of their teachers to prepare for administrative certification at a local college. Part of that preparation will include a full-time internship. If school districts are willing to spend a limited amount of money for paid internships, it will in the long run be an excellent investment for the future.[5]

It would seem from this chapter that the preparation needed to become an effective educational leader could take a lifetime. In fact, a superintendent must be a lifetime learner with a broad range of intellectual interests. No college program or set of certification requirements can guarantee that a man or woman is prepared for all of the challenges that a superintendent might face (table 2.1 summarizes the certification requirements for the fifty states and the District of Columbia). Still, a strong academic program, along with an effective internship, is very desirable. The other factor that will affect the success or failure of a school leader is the prior job experience the person brings to the position. The work that the individual has done before assuming the chief school officer's position might be crucial not only to obtaining the job but also to succeeding as a superintendent. We will examine the career patterns of those seeking the superintendency in the next chapter.

Table 2.1

Superintendent Certification Requirements

Teaching or Administrative Experience	Master's Degree and Graduate Study	Internship/ Previous Administrative Employment	Teaching Certification	Recommendation from Approved Institution
Alabama–3 years	Alaska	Alaska–1 year	Arkansas	Connecticut
Alaska–5 years	Arizona	Connecticut–30 months	California	Delaware
Arizona–3 years	Connecticut	Idaho–1 year	Missouri	Indiana
Arkansas–4 years	Delaware	Illinois–2 years	Montana	Missouri
California–3 years	District of Columbia	Iowa–3 years	North Dakota	Nebraska
Connecticut–80 months	Idaho	Kansas–3 years	Oklahoma	New Hampshire
District of Columbia–5 years	Illinois	Kentucky–2 years	Rhode Island	North Carolina
Idaho–4 years	Iowa	Louisiana–5 years	South Carolina	Pennsylvania
Indiana–5 years	Kansas	Maine–2 years	Tennessee	South Carolina
Kentucky–3 years	Kentucky	Maryland–2 years	Utah	Utah
Maine–3 years	Louisiana	Massachusetts–3 years	Wyoming	
Maryland–3 years	Maine	Minnesota–3 years		
Missouri–4 years	Maryland	Montana–1 year		
Montana–3 years	Massachusetts	New Hampshire–3 years		
Nebraska–2 years	Minnesota	New York–1 year		
Nevada–3 years	Missouri	North Carolina–1 year		
New York–3 years	Montana	North Dakota–4 years		
Oklahoma–1–2 years	Nebraska	Ohio–3 years		
Pennsylvania–6 years	Nevada	Utah–2 years		
Rhode Island–8 years	New Hampshire			
South Carolina–7 years	Indiana			
South Dakota–4 years	New York			
Tennessee–5 years	North Carolina			
Vermont–7 years	North Dakota			
Virginia–5 years	Oklahoma			
West Virginia–3 years	Pennsylvania			
Delaware–3 years	Rhode Island			
	South Carolina			
	South Dakota			
	Tennessee			
	Vermont			
	Virginia			
	Washington			
	West Virginia			
	Wisconsin			

Source: Joel E. Boydston, *Teacher Certification Requirements in All Fifty States* (Sebring: Teacher Certification Publications, 1998).

NOTES

1. E. Joseph Schneider, paper presented at the American Association of School Administrators Conference, February 1999, 2–3.

2. Schneider, 4.

3. J. Murphy and N. Shipman, "The Interstate School Leaders Licensure Consortium: A Standards-Based Approach to Strengthening Educational Leadership," AASA Online, <www.aasa.org/issues/leadership/murphy.htm> (1998).

4. Major John Stanford, *Victory in our Schools* (New York: Bantam, 1999), xvi.

5. *Rochester Democrat and Chronicle*, 12 February 2000.

CHAPTER THREE

Career Paths Leading to the Superintendency

Historically, most chief school officers began as teachers, went on to become building principals, and moved on to the superintendency. Some also served along the way in a central office position such as assistant superintendent. Most often, this progression took an individual into their forties before being appointed to his or her first superintendency. Those who earned a doctorate sometimes moved more quickly up the career ladder. Today, this pattern is being challenged by the desire of some boards of education to hire their chief school officers from outside the education system.

The long accepted idea that someone aspiring to the superintendency should first become a teacher is being challenged. Those who have favored teaching experience as a qualification for administration have argued that only someone who has worked in a classroom can possibly lead a school system. If we think of the superintendent's primary role as that of an instructional leader, it may seem inconceivable that a person without teaching experience could know enough about education to do the job. These individuals would suggest that it would be similar to having a managing partner in a law firm who had never studied or practiced law.

Still, the fact cannot be ignored that in recent years, a number of major districts have hired their superintendents from other fields. These districts have believed that managing a large school system is not significantly different than managing a business. For these board members, the primary role of the superintendent is to motivate and to manage. In these districts, the day-to-day curriculum and instructional issues are delegated to assistant superintendents and principals.

It has been the conventional wisdom that superintendents will be more effective educational leaders if they have had experience as teachers and as principals. Working as a principal also gives a person experience with working with unions, parents, and community groups. Still, it must be admitted that experience in the classroom or as a building principal does not in itself prepare someone to be a superintendent. The same can be said about working in a central office position. Assistant superintendents sometimes have little power to make independent decisions, and one might even argue that a building principal has more latitude in making choices than anyone in the central office, with the exception of the superintendent. All things being equal, it is hard to deny that experience in education is a positive factor in preparing someone to be a superintendent. In the past, traditionally prepared school administrators have been critical of the idea of bringing in an outsider to administer a school district.

More recently, there have been examples where this practice has been successful. As noted in chapter 2, John Stanford was a retired major general and county executive before being hired in Seattle as superintendent of schools. Stanford's work in Seattle was first given national recognition in a Public Broadcasting System special report entitled "Tale of Three Cities."[1] It told the story of how the charismatic Stanford was able to work effectively with the teacher's union and the community to bring about constructive change in a large urban district in just three years. A large number of news stories also reported the city's reaction when their superintendent became critically ill. This outpouring of sympathy and emotion emphasized the fact that a superintendent of schools can and often does have a tremendous impact on his or her community. Reading Stanford's book entitled *Victory in Our Schools* also caused many to admire his leadership in Seattle.

On the other hand, the same television program showed the trials and tribulations of David Hornbeck, who was hired in 1994 to lead the Philadelphia school district. Unlike Stanford, Hornbeck, a minister and a lawyer, antagonized the teachers of the city. His tenure seems to have been characterized primarily by strife and gridlock. Other cities have also looked outside education for their leadership. San Diego, for example, is led by a former federal prosecutor, while New Orleans has hired a retired marine colonel.

It is much too early to know whether this hiring pattern will grow and, more important, whether it will help school districts. A number of observers have suggested that hiring from outside the educational community would work best in a large district. Such an organization would have a sufficient administrative staff available to advise the superintendent. A smaller district in which the superintendent must indeed be the instructional leader should select someone who knows about teaching and learning.

Although the practice of hiring former business people or military officers as superintendents may offer a solution for some districts, it does not seem that it is a cure all for the problems of our public schools. On the other hand, it might be a practice with which we could experiment. This does not mean that we should allow local school boards to hire one of their own members or merely to select the owner of the local hardware store. Certification programs for superintendents should continue to be in place. A board of education seeking to hire someone other than a certified administrator should be required to obtain a waiver from the appropriate state agency. This request could be evaluated by an independent review board. Such a group could consider the credentials of the nominee, as well as the reasons for the request. A state that allows such waivers should be mandated to review periodically the success of the program. Although such an option will continue to be controversial, it probably will not become a major trend.

Most likely, future superintendents will continue to be selected from those who have worked in a school system. How best to devise a career path that will lead to the superintendency is a question open to differing opinions. Many believe that a future superintendent would be wise to teach and also to earn a master's degree before considering administration. The master's degree can be in any field related to education. Secondary teachers might well consider a degree in their subject area. Graduate programs in special education and reading could also be helpful to a future administrator. Another alternative would be a general education program in curriculum development. After earning this degree within the first three to five years of teaching, a future school administrator might be ready to consider the next step.

The first important decision is whether an aspiring superintendent should apply for a program leading only to certification or whether to seek a doctorate. Whichever choice is made, a person should carefully review the curricula and evaluate the reputation of the college programs in the area in which he or she lives. Often, spending the additional money to attend a more prestigious college or university is a good investment. The decision whether to seek a doctorate will depend on a number of factors. If a person's career plan includes working as a superintendent in a large suburban or urban district, the doctorate is extremely important. For smaller schools, it is seldom required. Several other issues should be considered, too. For instance, will it be possible to expend the money necessary to finance several years of additional study? There is also the question of whether a person has the time to complete a doctoral study. This issue is crucial as one considers family obligations, and it is imperative that the question of graduate study be thoroughly discussed within a family. A potential superintendent must also think about the effect that this commitment of time will have on his or her work as a teacher or administrator.

Once a person considering administration decides on the type of graduate program he or she will pursue, it is important to begin to plan a career path. Even prior to completing the requirements for administrative certification, a person should prepare to make the first move out of a classroom position. During this period, the future administrator should begin to build a résumé that will demonstrate leadership qualities. Acting as a committee chairperson of faculty groups and accepting leadership roles in the community can only enhance a résumé. Attending Parent Teacher Association meetings and other school functions will demonstrate that a teacher has interests beyond his or her own classroom. Involvement in professional groups within one's discipline, such as the county social studies council, can also be helpful. Although working within the teacher's union can offer a young teacher valuable experience, a person wishing to become an administrator in the district might be cautious about becoming an overly zealous union member. This is especially true where there is some animosity between the district and the teacher's union. Militant teacher's union leaders do not often become superintendents. If part-time roles as an elementary grade team leader or a department chairperson in the secondary school are available, the future administrator should seek out these jobs.

As one considers moving from a position as a full-time teacher, it is very helpful to have a mentor. Such a relationship can develop when a teacher seeking a career in administration shares this aspiration with a person currently in an administrative role. Often, the mentor will be the principal, but it can be anyone in the district who serves in a leadership position. As a friendship develops, the mentor not only can give useful advice but also becomes an advocate for the future administrator. Most people who have become administrators can look back on one or more people who have helped and encouraged them along the way.

By the age of thirty-five, an aspiring administrator should make his or her first move. In some situations, an appropriate vacancy may not exist. It might also become clear that those in power are not likely to promote an individual to any appropriate vacancy that does occur. It then becomes necessary to decide whether it is wise to move to another school to become a department chairperson or assistant principal. One should not wait too long as such a move could cause a prospective administrator to accept a reduced salary. Making a move can be a disruption in one's life, especially if a person has a spouse who is happy in his or her own position. Of course, taking children out of their schools can also be traumatic. These sorts of considerations are why it is best to make any moves early during one's career. It is much easier to make a change with a family made up of preschool children rather than adolescents. However difficult changing schools might be, it is often necessary for a person seeking to become a superintendent. Few superintendents are able to be promoted first from a teacher to a building principal and then to superintendent in the same district.

There is increasing discussion about the need for school districts to preselect and finance the preparation of their own future leaders. This practice may grow as districts have more and more difficulty finding qualified candidates. Prince George City, Maryland, superintendent Iris Metts is planning an effort "to grow superintendents through a superintendent's round table." At Maryland's Bowie State University, a doctoral program is being established for superintendents. A number of nearby school districts have committed to recommend students for the program.[2] Plans such as this, especially if school districts give them financial support, can create new opportunities for future superintendents.

Even with such programs, the fact remains that future school administrators may have to make several moves prior to being appointed to their first superintendency. Willingness to relocate will not in itself ensure that even an ambitious candidate will be given a chance at the top job in a district. Several factors will help a person move up the career ladder more quickly. First and foremost, an individual must be effective in every job listed on one's résumé. The Peter Principle states, "In a hierarchy, every employee tends to rise to his level of incompetence."[3] Whether or not Dr. Peter has it right, it must also be observed that people are not often promoted for doing a poor job in their current position. Despite the fact that it might be debated in some schools, most teachers who have become principals were at least competent in the classroom. It is also true that incompetent principals and assistant superintendents are not likely to be hired as chief school officers. Thus, the prospective administrator's first task is to prove effectiveness in the job from which he or she hopes to be promoted. Obviously, this is not enough, as our school systems contain many competent people.

Somehow, future administrators must demonstrate that they can lead. Proof of this skill will need to be evident in the candidate's résumé and recommendations. It is also necessary that the future administrator have a powerful group of references. These can include supervisors in the school,

college professors, clergymen, and members of the community. It is probably most convenient if these references are gathered in a college placement file. Since any recommendation that is not absolutely glowing can
be harmful to a candidate, it is essential that a person be as certain as possible that references are extremely positive. When requesting that someone write a recommendation, it is often a good idea to ask, "Could you
write a positive reference for me?"

Résumés are strengthened when they contain examples of presentations
that have been made at professional conferences. Having written articles
for educational publications might also be impressive to some potential
employers. So many conferences are held and educational publications
published that it is less difficult than one might think to become an authority. This is especially true if an administrator is able to develop a
unique program in his or her school.

Finally, a person wishing to become a superintendent cannot leave it to
chance. A great deal of luck will be involved, and one must be in the right
place at the right time. It is extremely important that when the opportunity
does arise, a candidate is prepared. Certification work should be done and
a person's placement file complete. One's family should be aware of a
person's career aspirations and know that these ambitions might well require a family to move to another community. A position as a superintendent of schools will most likely be offered to people who have prepared themselves for leadership. Is this position really worth all of the
effort and sacrifices a person might have to undergo to achieve an appointment? In chapter 4, I will address the key question concerning the
advantages and disadvantages of the position.

NOTES

1. *The Merrill Report*, 1999.
2. *USA Today*, 26 January 2000, 7(D).
3. Dr. Laurence J. Peter and Raymond Hull, *The Peter Principle* (New York: Bantam,
1969), front cover.

CHAPTER FOUR

Sacrifices and Rewards of the Position

Whatever path one follows to the superintendency, it is important to know in advance both the positive and negative aspects of the position. Even though there are many potential disadvantages to becoming a superintendent, collectively they still do not create a strong case for avoiding consideration of the job.

Perhaps the most common problem cited is that the job is an extremely high-stress position. There is no question that this is true. Because many individuals and groups are attempting to influence decisions within a school system, the superintendent will find that pressures emerge from multiple sources. If the district is considering changing from half-day kindergarten to full-day kindergarten, for example, parents will come out on both sides of the issue. Some disagreement among the faculty might also be expressed. The superintendent will be in a position to mediate these differences and to help find the best decision for the district. A current problem at the secondary level that is creating conflict in many districts is a move to block scheduling. Again, the superintendent needs to consider the feelings of parents, faculty, and students while considering such a program change. Contract negotiations with employee groups and budget battles can also increase the tension level in a district. Media criticism is always possible for a superintendent. A person who cannot accept public criticism should think twice about a major leadership position. There will doubtless be rancorous meetings, all-night bargaining sessions, and possibly even picket lines to pass through.

These experiences can have an effect on a superintendent's physical and mental health. On the other hand, such experiences are not inevitable, nor are they frequent for most superintendents. Many who have served as assistant principals and as building principals believe that these positions are actually more stressful on a day-to-day basis than the job of the superintendent. Being on the front lines dealing with student and faculty problems one after another leaves building administrators with very little time to sit back and plan or reflect on the future. Superintendents frequently have much more control over their schedules and also can delegate a number of the less important administrative tasks.

Of course, there are ways to alleviate the effects of stress. It is important to maintain a reasonable schedule that includes many evenings at home, rather than out at meetings. An administrator needs to have a life away from the office that allows the opportunity to focus on something other than the individual's job. Hobbies, spending time with family and friends, or teaching a college course are certainly possibilities. Daily physical activity is an effective way to deal with the pressure of the position. Still, a person who is seeking to have a life as free of conflict as possible should probably avoid the superintendency. On the other hand, not many jobs in our society today are stress-free. Certainly firefighters, fishermen, and farmers will also face periods of anxiety in their jobs. If a person is physically and mentally strong, most potential candidates will not find the pressures to be overwhelming.

One of the most important concerns a potential superintendent might have if he or she has a family is the effect of the job on the spouse and children. In 1998, a paper entitled "Private Lives of Public Leaders: A Spousal Perspective" was published on-line by the American Association of School Administrators. A total of 575 spouses of school administrators completed a survey on the effects of the job on the administrator's family.   Needless to say, the results included a number of negative effects. The spouse of an administrator in Nebraska commented, "I miss his companionship and feel lonely a lot.[1] A husband of an assistant superintendent wrote, "There is not much time left for us."[2] Other spouses reported that their partners were so tired from the job that they were uninterested in doing anything in the evenings at home. A frustrated wife wrote, "He falls asleep while watching television or reading. I often feel neglected because of the time commitment to the job." Another wrote that her husband had "a tendency to take out his frustrations at home." Many complained about the lack of contact with the children in the family. Still, it should be noted that in the same study, children of administrators were asked "how they liked being the child of a school administrator." Twenty-nine percent said they liked it very much, fifty-two percent said they liked it somewhat, fourteen percent did not like it much, and only three percent said they hated it.[3]

The problem of the impact on administrators' families cannot be minimized. The loneliness of the spouse also on occasion turns to anger when it appears that the administrator only seems to care about the job.

Birthdays and anniversary celebrations often have to be sacrificed to evening meetings. These problems can be disruptive to a family, and someone considering the superintendency must be aware that it is possible to allow the job to become too important and therefore adversely affect one's personal life.

To put the issue in perspective, it must be pointed out that to take on any important public position can produce similar pressures. Also, such pressures are not unique to the superintendency. A building principal can be away from his or her home as many evenings as the superintendent. In fact, in many communities, there is more pressure on a high school principal to be present at school events than the superintendent.

An essential question that will be dealt with later in this book is, How can superintendents balance their professional and personal lives? Many superintendents have found ways to do so and thus have reduced or eliminated the potential negative effects of the position on one's family. As evidence to this fact, a final statistic that turned up in the survey should be noted. Eighty-four percent of the respondents indicated that they liked being married to a school administrator. A superintendent's husband wrote, "She's great. Being a school administrator doesn't detract from her as a person. It just takes a little bit too much of her time at night."[4]

Another major concern with the position is that it lacks job security. Unlike most other professionals employed in school districts, superintendents in most states lack the protection of tenure. As a result, a chief school officer's continued employment by a school district is dependent on maintaining the support of a majority of the board of education. This could mean that a superintendent's contract might not be renewed if the board's support is not constant. To ensure that board members are happy also often requires that the superintendent is thought well of by school employees and members of the community. It is sometimes not difficult for a school district leader to lose support with one or more constituencies. In fact, sometimes no matter what decision a superintendent makes on an issue, it is inevitable that some people will be upset. Keeping employees, the board, and the community supportive is a challenge, especially when dealing with issues such as budget and contract negotiations.

It must be admitted that especially in our cities, superintendent turnover is unacceptably high. A person cannot easily bring about positive change in a school district in two or three years. New York City had twelve superintendents in twenty years, while Kansas City has gone through eighteen chief school officers in the last thirty years.[5] Although in suburban and rural districts, the average tenure is five to six years, still the high turnover rate continues to be a problem. Ninety-two percent of superintendents surveyed believed that "high turnover in the superintendency is a serious crisis in American education."[6]

Even though this turnover rate is a problem area, it is important to consider some of the reasons superintendents leave their positions. Often, people assume that superintendents always leave a district because they are forced out or because their position has become uncomfortable. Some of these situations are very unpleasant. The *Poughkeepsie Journal* recently featured an article demonstrating the conflicts that sometimes arise in school districts. A superintendent and an assistant superintendent who left their jobs in the Hyde Park, New York, School District were intending to sue the district for "intentional emotional distress and damage to their professional reputations."[7] Such an incident only highlights the potential conflicts that can occur between administrators and their boards of education.

On the other hand, if the superintendent is not being let go for moral or ethical reasons, there is every reason to believe that a chief school officer leaving a district will find other excellent employment opportunities. Some who have left have found positions in education, while a number have ended up in management positions in other fields.

A major factor to consider when studying the high turnover rates is that many superintendents are voluntarily moving to more lucrative superintendencies. Frequently, both the salary and prestige of a chief school officer's position are determined by the number of students attending district schools. Many superintendents feel that to improve their positions in the field, they must keep moving to larger and larger districts. Thus, a good deal of the turnover in the position is caused by the practice of superintendents moving to larger districts. Sometimes, superintendents make a final move simply to raise their salary to ensure a higher pension. Given all the reasons that superintendents have for leaving their positions, job security should not be considered a major detriment for someone considering the position. In a later chapter, we will discuss how superintendents can have long and fulfilling careers in a district. If that is one's goal, it is not an "impossible dream."

A frequently stated argument against becoming a superintendent is that a person never has any real contact with children. A comment has often been made along these lines. "I went into education to help children, and I can't do that sitting in meetings all day in the central office." Although a superintendent will have less daily contact with children than does a teacher or principal, chief school officers do not need to spend all or most of their time in the central office. An effective superintendent should frequently be in schools with students and faculty. Lack of visibility within the schools is often a major criticism of superintendents. Having lunch with students and faculty is one way to increase visibility. Attendance and participation in school events is another obvious way to be involved. Judging science fairs, sitting in with the school band, and actively participating in teacher conferences are also ways to become engaged with teachers and students. Formal and informal classroom visits and simply talking to students and teachers can only help superintendents be more effective leaders.

Although it is seldom practiced today, some administrators do find time to actually teach in a classroom. This could include teaching a class that meets at 8:00 in the morning or working as part of a teaching team at an elementary grade level. Other superintendents make it a practice to seek invitations to be guest speakers in classrooms. It is also an excellent idea to advertise the fact that the superintendent is available as a judge for science fairs or speech contests. One superintendent even made it a practice to serve as a lunchroom monitor. If a superintendent is isolated from children and the learning process, it is not because it is inevitable. One has to make frequent visits to schools a top priority. As the chief school officer, a person will to a large extent have control over his or her own schedule.

Even if a superintendent spends little or no time in the schools, it still cannot be said that the chief school officer of a district has little or no effect on how children are learning. The fact is that the decisions made by a superintendent will have immense impact on what goes on in schools. Perhaps most important is the power to recommend to the board the teachers who will be working in the classrooms. In addition, the superintendent will be extremely important in policy, budget, and curriculum decisions. To suggest that a superintendent's work does not affect children is just not true. A truly effective superintendent should be the chief advocate for the young people attending district schools. In fact, the position offers the opportunity to positively influence the lives and education of every child.

It has often been said that superintendents are bound to be lonely people. The conventional wisdom is that the boss can have no real friends within the organization. Unquestionably the superintendent has to maintain a certain formality with employees. It is not likely that someone in the position is going to be able to share personal problems with a subordinate in the organization. The role demands a certain level of aloofness. Of course, this need is true in any organization, but it certainly does not eliminate the possibility of personal friendships. Often, the superintendent will become close to other individuals by acting as a mentor. In any case, a successful superintendent will develop meaningful relationships within the organization and learn to care about fellow employees sincerely. A certain "loneliness at the top" does exist, but a superintendent will always have family and friends who are not connected with the job. A superintendent does not have to feel isolated from fellow human beings if he or she is willing to develop meaningful friendships.

A related problem is that in many areas some negative feelings persist about school administrators. Some citizens believe there are just too many administrators, suggesting that the best way to improve schools is to get rid of some of the "worthless, overpaid administrators." In many school districts where superintendent and principal salaries may be among the highest in the community, a certain level of resentment is evident. In California, these feelings have led to laws limiting the number of administrators. Another result has been a trend to cap administrative salaries. These feelings in a school district are not inevitable; many school administrators are popular and effective community leaders. These individuals are able to earn the affection and respect of citizens, staff, and the student body.

Thus far in this chapter, we have dealt with the potential drawbacks of the position of the superintendency, but one can argue equally that a number of important reasons might lead a person to consider such a role. *USA Today* used as a page one feature story an article entitled "Superintendents in Demand." It cited a study done by Fordam University describing the typical superintendent as a middle-aged white male who serves in the position a little over seven years and plans to retire at age fifty-seven. The average age of superintendents is now fifty-two, and it is inevitable that the large number of current vacancies will only increase. The problem of attracting qualified candidates is present in all types of districts.[8] The exodus of superintendents, along with the reluctance of most teachers and principals to even seek the position, almost guarantee unparalleled opportunities for future candidates.

If the field is more open than in recent times, the financial incentives have never been better. Average salaries of chief school officers have increased dramatically during the last decade. In a survey conducted during the 1998–99 school year, the average salary reported among districts of all sizes was more than $106,000 per year.[9] High-paying suburban districts are now giving salaries that have gone beyond $200,000 annually. Dan Domenech, the superintendent in Fairfax County, Virginia, recently agreed to a salary of $205,000 per year.[10]

In many states, pension benefits based on these salaries will be very generous. The fact that superintendents most often retire at a young age speaks to the financial security that is offered by their pensions. Those superintendents who wish to continue working will find many opportunities at colleges, acting as interim administrators and consultants. Even though these positions may not always be highly paid, with retirement benefits a superintendent can often increase his or her income after leaving the position. A superintendent's contract also often provides funds to allow travel and additional in-service opportunities. In addition, districts frequently provide health and life insurance benefits for their superintendents. With the increased demands for superintendents, fringe benefits and salaries are likely to become even more attractive.

Opportunities and financial advantages are not alone strong enough reasons for pursuing a position as a superintendent. More important is the fact that it is an extremely challenging and exciting career. While many people are bored with a job that has unending repetition, a superintendent seldom experiences days that are exactly the same.

Finally, the most important reason for considering this leadership position is that it can make a difference in many people's lives. As a chief school officer, it is possible to help make your community a better place. Great satisfaction is derived from projects that improve instruction for children and from the knowledge that children, faculty, and the community feel positively about the school system.

When the time comes for a superintendent to retire, it is possible to look back with pride on what has been accomplished. It might be new buildings that have been built, teachers and administrators who have been hired, or new programs that have been instituted. Positive feelings expressed by students, staff, parents, and board members when one finally does retire from the position will provide pleasant memories to be treasured for a lifetime. As with any job, there will be times when the position will be very difficult. Still, most retired superintendents look back on their careers with pride and many happy memories.

If the reader has not yet given up on the possibility of pursuing a career as a chief school officer, I now would like to devote much of the remainder of this book to suggest some ways that one might succeed in the position.

NOTES

1. Martha Bruckner, "Private Lives of Public Leaders: A Spousal Perspective," AASA Online, www.aasa.org/sa/June9803.htm (1998).

2. Bruckner, "Private Lives of Public Leaders," 3.

3. Bruckner, "Private Lives of Public Leaders," 5.

4. Bruckner, "Private Lives of Public Leaders," 6.

5. *USA Today*, 26 January 2000, 1(A).

6. *USA Today*, 26 January 2000, 2(A).

7. *Poughkeepsie Journal,* 30 January 2000, 1.

8. *USA Today*, 26 January 2000, 2(A).

9. "What's a Superintendent Make?" AASA Online, www.aasa.org/issues/careeradv/career3.htm (1998).

10. "What's a Superintendent Make?"

CHAPTER FIVE

The First Year

The 1992 Clinton campaign developed a slogan to keep the campaign focused. They were constantly reminding each other, "It's the economy, stupid!" For a new superintendent it seems that the slogan should be "It's the people, stupid!" The first weeks in a new job should be a time of meeting and listening to people. This means really listening and, when appropriate, actually taking notes. People know whether an individual is really listening and concerned about what they are saying, and most appreciate a person in authority who does something besides talking. It goes without saying that a superintendent needs to have an understanding of the school and community. This type of understanding can best be gained by getting out of the office and hearing what others think the priorities of the district should be.

After beginning with individual conversations with his or her personal staff, a new superintendent should spend time with faculty members, nonteaching staff, students, and community members. At a conference, the director of the Office of Teacher Certification of New York State commented publicly that the new commissioner of education, Richard Mills, was the first commissioner ever to enter the Office of Teacher Certification. Not only did the new commissioner ask numerous questions, but he also followed up the visit with a memo that helped bring about needed changes in the office. Such follow-up notes are an added indication that an administrator is indeed listening. It is important that any written commendation be specific and not appear to be a form letter.

A new superintendent must also take the time to visit schools and interact informally with the students and faculty. When one observes something positive, compliment the staff member or send a personal note. Copies of such notes should be sent to the employee's supervisor and included in the individual's personnel file. On the other hand, where a problem surfaces, a superintendent should first work with the person's supervisor to resolve the issue informally. It is also essential to meet people in the community. It should be made public knowledge that the superintendent is eager to meet with community groups. Additionally, it is important to take every opportunity for informal discussions with citizens.

People will be eager to know the vision for the district, but it might be best to be cautious about articulating specific programs until a superintendent has a more complete impression of the attitudes and priorities of the different interest groups in the community. Even though a superintendent's public comments are of a general nature, it is essential to prepare carefully for any speaking assignment or meeting. First impressions are extremely important.

The groups that the superintendent will spend the most time with are the board of education and fellow district administrators, but it is still important to understand that one's ultimate success will depend on maintaining an acceptable level of trust and support from the various contingencies in the school district. In bringing about positive change and avoiding the gridlock that often develops in school districts, a chief school officer must establish reliable lines of communication with all of those who attempt to effect school policy. Building these relationships, whether it be with the PTA or the Sports Booster Club, is time-consuming but essential. The goal should be to reach the point where frank discussions can take place with the key leaders in the district. This is especially true with the presidents of the board of education and the teachers association. Equally important is the need to develop a sense of mutual trust and loyalty with the administrators and secretaries of the district. These people will require constant support and need to know that the superintendent is truly concerned about them and their work.

Thus, during the early days, a new administrator should be meeting with many people and listening carefully. It is even possible to set up specific times and days to talk to the public. This can be done either in the school or in another public building. Evenings can be spent reading policy manuals, contracts, and recent board minutes, but during the day, a new superintendent's time should be used to learn as much as possible. It is quite possible that as a new superintendent, a person comes to a district with an agenda in mind. It will be much easier to plan tactics for effective change if the new superintendent understands the "current climate" in the school and community. It is also possible that as a result of listening to others, initial ideas and plans will need to be modified.

Another important need is to learn as much as possible about those individuals who served as superintendent in the district in recent years. What were their perceived strengths and weaknesses? Without a doubt, a new chief school officer will be compared with them. This comparison is especially difficult if a person is following a popular superintendent. In any case, it is best to compliment the accomplishments of the people who held the position in the past. If these individuals are available, seeking their guidance is certainly appropriate. Whatever the reputation of those who served in the past, it is important to avoid being critical of them. Comments, whether private or public, should demonstrate that the new superintendent does not engage in idle gossip and that his or her true concern is not the mistakes of the past but what is best for the children of the district in the future.

There will be many meetings to attend during those first weeks on the job. Prior to meeting any group, it is important to determine exactly what the objectives are for the session. Remember, people expect the superintendent to be articulate and well organized. One cannot afford to be perceived as anything less than the educational leader of the community. As a leader, it is important to model the type of professional discourse that should be maintained in the district. The intellectual respect that others develop for a superintendent is at least as important as the desire to be seen as a "regular person." Still, especially with community groups, it is essential to avoid as much as possible the jargon of the profession. Speeches and meetings with the public will offer opportunities to be both a teacher and a leader. One of the biggest mistakes a superintendent can make is to take public appearances too lightly. Most superintendents can speak quite easily in any setting, but it is very easy to get into trouble if an individual speaks without adequate thought or preparation.

In conclusion, the first weeks on the job should allow people to see their new superintendent at his or her very best. Most individuals will be friendly, especially if a person is perceived as being concerned and open. During these early days it is good to remember "It is the people, stupid!" Listen and be positive in comments to others. Make notes and seek to remember as much as possible (especially names) about new individuals. A seating chart of those individuals who are present at a meeting is helpful. This helps an administrator to remembering their names, both during the meeting and in the future.

All of these meetings and discussions should help a new administrator devise a plan for improving the district and also aid in the development of a strategy for implementing those goals that emerge. It is essential not to attempt to do too much too quickly, and people must understand that their input is being utilized to construct the priorities for the district.

During a superintendent's first weeks in the district, he or she will be asked frequently to speak publicly. It is important that during these opportunities the superintendent becomes a spokesperson for the children. Faculty and staff must see the chief school officer as more than the "mouthpiece" of the board of education. At the same time, the board of education should know that their superintendent is concerned about the faculty and staff but that his or her most important loyalty is to the children of the district. These objectives can be best met if one prepares carefully for meetings and public appearances. During an administrator's "honeymoon" period, he or she must seek to be a caring, concerned individual who is willing to listen and also someone who doesn't spend most of the day behind closed doors. This initial time in a new job will set the tone for an administrator's entire career in the district.

Once a new superintendent has begun to feel comfortable with those around him or her and has listened to the concerns of all segments of the school and community, it is time to develop plans for the future of the district. Reaching this point will probably take most of the first semester in a new job. However long it takes, the weeks used being a listener and a learner will have been time well spent. This period should give some strong indications as to the answers to the following questions:

1. What are the problems of the district as perceived by board members, administrative staff, faculty, nonteaching personnel, students, parents, and community members? What do these groups perceive as the district's strengths?
2. What programs do these individuals see as being necessary to deal with the perceived problems?
3. Are there common themes of agreement on any of the problems and solutions that have been suggested?
4. As a result of preliminary discussions, what are the pressing needs of the district?
5. Are there any obvious short- and long-term solutions to these dilemmas?

As a new superintendent considers the answers to these questions, some issues will quickly stand out—including anything from excessive class sizes to buildings badly in need of repair. Other issues might be people problems, such as poor morale or inadequate leadership. Such an issue could be dealt with quickly and easily, but some problems could take years to remedy. Because the individuals consulted within the district have seen potential problems from their own personal and limited perspectives, it may well be that the problem they have identified is really different than the one suggested. They might conclude, for instance, that although almost everyone is doing his or her job from day to day, no one has attempted to create a commitment to school improvement. The issues might also point toward a lack of focus or a failure to articulate a vision.

Prior to preparing one's first budget, it would be appropriate to share any observations with the administrative team. Such a meeting would provide the opportunity to share tentative conclusions that have been made concerning long- and short-range needs of the district. After receiving the input of fellow administrators, the superintendent could hold a similar discussion with the board of education. At this stage, the discussion should still be centered on problems or needs rather than solutions. When the board has reached a consensus on the future needs of the district, it will be time to consider the next step. If the district has no mission or philosophy statement, producing such a statement might be necessary at this point prior to entering into long-term planning.

Creating objectives and plans must be a collaborative process. The superintendent will be the person who will most often articulate the goals of the district, but in establishing these goals and the plans to implement them, it is necessary to include participants from all of the school constituencies. As the problem areas have already been identified, the task will now be to devise some measurable objectives. During these discussions, it is necessary to write a manageable number of long-term objectives (three to five years). In doing so, every effort should be made to make these goals specific and measurable. For instance, a target could be that within five years, ninety-five percent of all elementary students will be reading at or above grade level as measured by a specific standardized test. If this is a long-range goal, a separate column should be included that outlines the specific objective for the coming year. This first-year target might be to have ninety percent of all first grade students reading at or above grade level.

Using this example, discussion would then follow on how best to achieve the objective. With an instructional objective such as this, the primary dialogue would be with teachers. This discussion would include a careful examination of the research dealing with reading improvement. Consultants might be brought in, and teachers could be encouraged to visit schools that have successful programs. In any case, once the objective has been agreed on, a long- and short-range plan would have to be devised. With the objective to improve reading scores, the plan would need to be written in conjunction with budget preparations for the coming year.

The solution coming out of the planning meetings might include reducing class size in the first grade, hiring teacher aides, fostering staff development, or purchasing new materials. If the board and faculty agree with the objective, it can be given a high priority as the budget is prepared.

These objectives should also be tied to the district supervision program. Principals who are evaluated in part based on their success in meeting district objectives will work hard to achieve the desired outcomes. Rather than having a checklist or a report card–like evaluation system, it might be preferable to have a narrative report written at the end of each year. The narrative would be written based on how well the administrator had succeeded in meeting the previously agreed upon objectives. Every year in the summer the superintendent can sit with each administrator and together devise a list of three or four challenging but fair objectives for the coming twelve months. At least some of these objectives would be tied directly to the district's long- and short-range plans. A midyear progress conversation could take place in January, and in the spring the administrator could submit a written account of what had been accomplished with each of the agreed-on objectives. At a year-end evaluation conference, the superintendent and the administrator could discuss the progress and talk about the objectives for the coming year. Following this meeting, the superintendent might prepare a narrative evaluation of the administrator's work for the past year. Such a system focuses on what is being evaluated on the district's objectives.

If a school system already has an evaluation instrument in effect for administrators, it might not be easy to change it during a new superintendent's first year on the job. Once trust is developed, one's fellow administrators might well welcome a plan that is tied to district objectives. If the superintendent's personal evaluation format is also related to the objectives, it will be easier to convince other administrators that this is a positive way to improve the program. The most positive aspect of such a plan is that all objectives are mutually agreed on by the superintendent and his or her fellow administrators prior to the beginning of the school year.

In working with teachers, administrators hopefully could follow the same pattern. If the district objective at the time is to ensure computer literacy among the faculty, each teacher could be asked to take this on as a personal objective. Like that of the superintendent and the administrators, a teacher's annual review could also refer to the district objectives. The same approach can be used with nonteaching staff. If it is an objective to keep the buildings free of graffiti, this goal could be used in evaluating all cleaning personnel.

Using evaluations is only one way of carrying out district objectives. Eventual success depends in large part on devising a workable plan. Once we know what needs to be accomplished, it is essential that we examine carefully any research related to the objective. Many ways are being touted to improve student learning, and books and conferences abound on multiple intelligence, brain research, learning styles, and block scheduling. These and other solutions must be considered in light of what research has proven will be effective. All too often, schools have jumped on bandwagons only to find that the newest fad did not really change very much. In studying the alternatives, the superintendent must be a leader. Despite heavy pressure to move in a particular direction, a chief school officer should demand proof that a particular plan can make a difference. In examining alternatives, local university professors can sometimes offer assistance. The Internet is also a vast new source for educational research. Before embarking on a major program such as block scheduling or inclusion, the superintendent must be convinced that such an initiative will improve student learning in the district.

If, as the leader of the district, the superintendent is not completely committed to a plan of action, he or she will most likely be a less than convincing advocate. A new superintendent will always be under pressure to "make things happen," but without commitment and a well-thought-out plan, failure is more than likely. During one's first year, a new superintendent has listened and reacted and must now be ready to move forward. This creates the need to begin to share with the faculty, staff, and community the new administrator's vision for the future of the district. If one's preparation has been carefully done, these ideas will have already been the topic of discussion with groups and individuals in the school district. The objectives that have emerged from these conversations will have been contributed to by many. It is now the responsibility of the superintendent to convince the entire community that these are worthy objectives and that everyone's help is needed to achieve the desired ends. Whether the plans include reorganization, changing curriculums, or a building project, people must be persuaded that this is the right course for the district. Making the case for a proposed change is one of the main functions of leadership.

Hopefully, by the end of the first year a new administrator will have developed a level of trust with the various groups in the district and will be seen as a true advocate for children. The reputation that has evolved during the first twelve months will be difficult to alter, so it is necessary to avoid serious errors during this crucial period. Even if one has survived and prospered during these early months, it must be understood that the real work has just begun. At some point, it will be clear to any superintendent that the "honeymoon" period in a new district has come to an end. Even when one begins to experience criticism, it cannot be allowed to deter a superintendent from moving forward to carry out district objectives. One of the most important ways to accomplish the established goals is to develop a budget that includes sufficient financial support for these objectives.

CHAPTER SIX

Budgets and Bond Issues

Superintendents worry a great deal about budgets and bond issues. Most chief school officers consider a rejection of either a budget or bond issue as a personal defeat, especially in states where citizens vote on the budget each year. The fact is that very few chief school officers avoid the experience of having the voters defeat an initiative put forward by the district. At times, such setbacks can be difficult to accept, even though the conditions were such that success was unlikely. Some communities have a history of turning down almost all proposals. Superintendents in such districts have an even greater challenge in preparing such projects. Whatever the prospects are in the community for success or failure, it remains the superintendent's primary responsibility to prepare the best possible annual budgets and special bond issue options.

There are many ways to put together a school budget proposal, but certain factors need to be considered. Even though there is no "right way" for every community, the following process might offer some guidelines to a new administrator.

1. The first step should be to develop a budget calendar with dates beginning in the fall and ending with the adoption of the budget. This calendar should include the task, the person or persons responsible for carrying out the task, and a date for completion.
2. Next a list of district objectives should be prepared. As noted in the last chapter, this list should include both long- and short-range goals, and input should be sought from everyone in the organization. Again, the purpose of establishing objectives prior to constructing a budget is to ensure that the spending plan reflects the agreed-on aims of the district. Goals that are not given high priority in the budget are less likely to be accomplished.

3. In the fall, the superintendent and/or the business official need to project the budget for the coming year. Using their best estimate, they can begin by preparing a revenue project. Realizing that there is no way in October to pinpoint a fund balance, state aid, or a property tax increase, a superintendent can at least get a general total of the amount of money that might be available for the new budget. Once a projection of revenue is completed, a similar attempt can be made on forecasting expenditures. In many cases, this might include merely using the present rate of inflation and, for salaries, projecting what might be paid out to current staff. Looking at the agreed-on objectives, the administration can move some funds into the areas that will help meet district priorities. The result of this process will be a tentative dollar total for each portion of the budget. Once a balanced budget has been achieved, the superintendent can share the results with the administrative team.

4. The principals and other district managers should then be given a budget booklet containing the mission statement of the district and the agreed-on objectives for the coming year. They should also be given a total dollar figure that should not be exceeded. In addition, the booklet should ask them to submit a priority "wish list" of items they were unable to include in their budget request. Giving them a maximum figure to work with will avoid most of the painful cuts that would be necessary later on in the process, and it will also save everyone a lot of time in the weeks before the budget adoption. As part of the booklet, they should be given a separate page for every budget code in their area of responsibility. Prepared by the business office, these pages should include a description of the code, a five-year history of expenditures in the code, and a place to write their requests for the coming year. Most of the page should be used for the administrator to justify the proposed expenditure and the calculations made to arrive at the figure. In secondary schools, individual teacher budgets can be distributed and department budgets developed. At the elementary school level it can be done by grade levels. The codes assigned to principals should include categories such as instructional supplies, equipment, textbooks, and office supplies.

5. While budget requests are being completed, the superintendent and/or the business official will have their own booklet to complete. Their categories should include
   a. all salaries,
   b. fringe benefits,

c. debt payment,

d. insurance, and

e. other miscellaneous categories affecting the total school district.

The superintendent will also have to be responsible for the estimates of revenue. The head of the maintenance department should ask for input for potential projects from all administrators prior to completing the budget booklet. The final priority list of maintenance projects will be determined by the superintendent with the approval of the board of education. Additional codes that could be given to a complete maintenance supervisor might include

a. utilities,

b. maintenance and custodial supplies and equipment,

c. contracted services, and

d. emergency funds for unforeseen maintenance problems.

At the same time, the supervisor of transportation should be assigned the appropriate codes for the transportation responsibilities of the district.

On an established date at the beginning of the new year, all budget booklets should be given to the superintendent. A new updated revenue projection is made, and the budget should then be brought into balance. At this point, this first draft should be discussed and amended at a meeting of all administrators. At this meeting the administrators can attempt to convince the group why they need more money to meet the objectives of the district. Hopefully, an administrative consensus will evolve. If it does not, the superintendent will need to make the necessary decisions to ensure that a balanced budget proposal is ready for the board of education.

It is possible to have a board of education budget committee involved in these early stages. Such a committee can participate in establishing the district objectives and discussing an acceptable tax rate increase. If the committee wishes to be more active, it can hold hearings to listen to presentations by administrators and department heads. One should be cautioned against trying to involve the board members in too much detail. Such a committee is not necessary and may not be advisable or needed in your district. The same is true with a budget committee made up of citizens. Establishing such a group can help gain support for the budget, but it also can have the opposite effect.

6. A special board meeting can be held to review the first draft of the budget. The superintendent might consider having the administrative

team work together on this presentation. This should only be done if a comfortable consensus has been reached and the superintendent is confident that the administrators can effectively present and defend their section of the budget.

7. Several opportunities for the public to be heard can become part of the budget schedule. One public hearing could be held early in the budget process to give interested citizens an opportunity to express their priorities and concerns. At a public hearing, even though a tentative budget should be shared with the citizens present, the board and the administration can give the public the opportunity to recommend changes.

   Both the public and the members of the board of education will observe the superintendent very carefully at these meetings. The following factors might be considered as a superintendent participates in public meetings:

   a. The presentation should be clear and understandable to the public; handouts and/or visual aids should be used.
   b. Presentations at public meetings do not have to be made solely by the superintendent. Including board members as part of the presentation can be very helpful.
   c. The superintendent must be well prepared and have appropriate staff available to help answer questions.
   d. If the superintendent is unsure about a question, he or she should ask for additional time to obtain the facts. "Shooting from the hip" at a public meeting can cause great difficulty. A chief school officer can expect to be quoted in the school and community; therefore, it is important to be extremely careful with comments made at a public meeting.
   e. Remain as calm as possible. Antagonistic taxpayers may be present, and they may criticize district policies or make personal attacks. A superintendent's salary and contract could be a topic of conversation. It is important to decide in advance how one will deal with salary-related questions, but remember that if citizens want salary information, they can obtain it.

8. Written communications to the public about the budget are also very important. A detailed press release can be prepared for local newspapers that reflects a thoughtful description of the proposed budget. Many local newspapers lack the capability of doing anything beyond printing a press release. In any case, the superintendent needs to work with local reporters to ensure positive press coverage. When

reporters write a good story about the school, don't be afraid to compliment them. Reporters seldom get positive feedback and often appreciate a sincere compliment. Working with the press is an important part of an administrator's job, and the board and other administrators should understand that on topics such as the budget, the superintendent will be the chief spokesperson for the district.

In addition to the information that appears in the local newspapers, the administration will need to describe the budget in the regular school district newsletter or in a special mailing. What is given to the voters to read about the budget is critical. It is not necessary or advisable to send each voter a line item budget, although these must be available in the district office. The budget publication should begin with a summary in a letter or column with the signature or byline of the board president. This approach is especially helpful if the person is a trusted member of the community. Most superintendents favor a written presentation that includes general categories of the budget. It should compare revenues and expenditures in the proposed budget with those same categories the previous year. It is helpful to include graphs or charts along with pictures of children and staff members. The advantage of having the budget presentation as part of a newsletter is that it can also include some "good news stories" about what is happening in the district.

For many voters, the primary area of interest will be budget increases and how the increases will affect their property taxes. The sections of the publication explaining these figures should be carefully worded. Because it will probably be impossible to predict exactly the impact of the budget on individual tax bills, the district will have to qualify any statement. It would be a good idea to speak with an experienced superintendent on how to deal with this delicate issue.

9. Whether the public votes on the final budget or it merely needs board adoption, any information released to the public should emphasize the positive steps forward that the budget will make possible. During the process of determining the final budget, compromises will be necessary. The superintendent's goal must be to obtain the unanimous support of the board for any budget or proposed project. Anything less than unanimity could well mean conflict as the spending plan is made public.

10. A superintendent should be concerned with several special constituencies in gaining support for a budget or bond issue. It is important to develop an ongoing relationship with senior citizens
in the district. If they are organized, the superintendent should
meet with them periodically and not just when the district is
looking for their support. A senior citizen volunteer program can
be established in the schools. For very little lost revenue, a district can make available a senior citizen pass for school events.
A Grandparents' Day in the elementary school is also a popular
event. One very successful program some school districts have
implemented is to allow senior citizens to use the school halls
for walking before classes in the morning. Many find this preferable to walking in the local malls. Community education programs designed especially for senior citizens that take advantage
of a computer room or swimming pool are also helpful in building goodwill. Continuing education classes are a useful activity
for citizens of all ages. Opening schools in the evening for aer-
obics or Spanish classes will help potential voters identify with
the school. Do not forget about high school students who have
reached their eighteenth birthday. The superintendent can explain the budget in a senior social studies class. It is a mistake to
assume that these young people will not vote or that they will
necessarily support the budget. Along with these groups, it
should be known that the superintendent or another member of
the administrative team would be willing to discuss the budget
with any community group.

If, despite all of this hard work, the budget or bond issue fails, do not
despair. When it becomes necessary to react to defeat with the press, one
should avoid appearing angry or overly disappointed. Initially, the superintendent will probably need to defer detailed comments on the loss of a
referendum until after the board of education has met.

Special attention is necessary regarding the method of gaining approval
for a major bond issue. These initiatives are usually necessary when a district needs to borrow a significant amount of money to finance a major
project. The proposals most often include constructing new buildings or
renovating existing structures.

Planning such a project requires a significant amount of preparation.
Here are some of the steps that a school district might consider:

1. The first step entails appointment of faculty, staff, and citizen committees to discuss the problems facing the district. If the issue is over-
   crowded schools and additions or new buildings are to be considered,
   it is important to gain input from both district employees and members
   of the community. A district can consider having separate committees
   or creating a combined group. Any committees that are formed must be
   clearly advised as to the specific mission of the group. A well-thought-
   out mission statement is essential. Along with a mission statement,
   there should be a list of guidelines for the committee. A district should
   consider providing at least a minimal budget for advisory committees,
   even if it just for refreshments for their meetings. Any financial commitment demonstrates that the district considers the task of the group
   important. Most important, the mission statement must indicate that the
   group's financial report is to be considered advisory. In fact, it is often
   wise to call the group an "advisory committee." The superintendent
   and the board must maintain the power to make the final decision on
   what should be included in the bond issue. They also should be responsible for the decision on the timing for the vote.
2. During this preparation stage, the district should also consider employing a consultant to help frame the alternatives. This consultant
   can and should be made available to any advisory committee.
3. The financial planning for a bond issue is a very specialized task.
   Unless the school attorney has been through the process before, it
   would be wise to consider the employment of a specialized financial
   consultant. This person would help with both the planning process
   and the actual sale of the bonds. Even if a consultant is selected, the
   school attorney will still have to be involved in the legal work connected with the project.
4. During the preparation stage, the board should also weigh the possible advantage of having one or more public hearings. These meetings would allow citizens to share their opinions and concerns before a final plan is agreed on.
5. When the committee's work is complete and the board finalizes the
   details for the bond issue, it should be well publicized in the district.
   The local media should be sent detailed press releases, and a mailing should be made to all households in the district.
6. The superintendent and perhaps board members should make it known
   that they are available to speak about the plan at local meetings. Members of the advisory committee should be kept informed and if possible included in the campaign to gain support for the program. This is

especially true if these individuals have a high level of credibility in the district. A trusted community leader appearing with the superintendent at a local Kiwanis club meeting can only help the cause.

7. If public opposition to the plan arises, ways must be found to respond to any criticism. Additional press releases and possibly mailings might be necessary to thwart rumors or untrue public statements by the opposition.

Even well-planned campaigns can fail. The chief school officer must remember that defeated initiatives are part of being a superintendent and that he or she is not the first or last administrator to experience frustration and disappointment. After a period of reflection, the superintendent and the board of education will need to seek another way to deal with the problems that necessitated the bond issue. Through these difficult days, a superintendent must maintain a steady countenance and not be seen as someone who has been defeated.

Of course, the elation of victory will be followed by a long and difficult period of supervising the project approved by the voters. A number of factors need to be considered in carrying out a building program:

1. An architect may have been chosen prior to the vote. Whenever and however this decision is made, it must be done carefully. If the district has a well-qualified advisory committee, they can be given the initial task of screening architectural firms. This is usually done in meetings where a representative of the firm makes a presentation to the committee. A key aspect of the selection process is checking the references of the competing firms and perhaps viewing some of their previous work. In most districts, the superintendent becomes involved in this process by calling other chief school officers who have worked with the firms. Even if an advisory committee participates in screening the architects, the final decision must be with the superintendent and the board of education.

2. On most large projects, the school district should consider employing an independent clerk of the works to represent the school during the construction phase. This person should be a professional clerk who will be present on the site throughout the project. The primary role of a clerk of the works is to be the eyes and ears of the district and to ensure that the plans are followed. The clerk and the superintendent or his or her representative should be present at all of the meetings of the various contractors during the project.

3. During the course of construction undoubtedly a number of problems will arise. There will be construction difficulties that were unforeseen by the architect. Decisions will have to be made that could create the need for "change orders." These alterations in the original plans almost always mean additional expenses for the district. The superintendent of schools must stay abreast of these problems. Some contingency funds will be planned in the project, but without careful monitoring, major cost overruns can occur. This outcome can be a disaster for the project and could spell serious difficulties for the superintendent, who is ultimately responsible for managing the construction budget. It is essential that board members be kept informed concerning any serious problems that occur during the project. Where there are decisions that could have significant consequences, the board should be allowed to participate.

It is exciting to watch an addition or a new building go up in a school district. Such a project can be a source of pride to a superintendent, but if it is not carefully planned and carried out, the project can be a nightmare. Like any other aspect of administration, choosing the right people to carry out the work is all important. The superintendent should be the key individual in choosing those who will have the primary responsibility for carrying out the project.

Planning and administering bond issues and annual budgets are important aspects of the superintendent's job. In carrying out these duties, it is imperative to work carefully with the individuals in the business department and also with the independent auditor. The individual or firm that audits the district's financial records is often an excellent source of advice. Individuals working in the business office must not only be competent but also loyal and trustworthy. Although these people are important in carrying out the day-to-day financial transactions, it is necessary to remember that the superintendent is the one responsible for how district funds are expended. When there are mistakes, the chief school officer must be willing to take the blame. If the business aspect of schools has not been a priority in your past experience, take the time to learn and become involved. To do less would be neglect of duty.

When making the important financial decisions of the district, the superintendent will be working very closely with the board of education. Maintaining an appropriate relationship with this group of people is absolutely essential to the success of any administrator. It is to this all-important subject that we turn next.

CHAPTER SEVEN

The Superintendent's Relationship with the Board of Education

As a new superintendent, one will begin with the advantage of working with board of education members who have been involved in the appointment process. Most of them are likely to be eager that their new superintendent succeed. Because of the rapid turnover of board members, an administrator may not have this luxury for many years. As a result, a superintendent's relationship with board members is a dynamic one, and sometimes the changes are dramatic. The board of education's support for a superintendent can never be taken for granted. This is illustrated by the old story of the superintendent who was taken suddenly to the hospital and several days later received the following note from the board: "In your absence, at a recent meeting the following resolution was approved. Resolved that—the Board of Education extends to the superintendent its best wishes for a rapid and speedy recovery." Below the resolution, it was noted that the vote was four to three.

To work effectively with a board of education, one must understand its legal responsibilities. A school board is a public corporate body. In many ways, it is identical to the board of directors of a local bank or Ford Motor Company. Like a corporation, a board has a chief executive officer who is the superintendent. A single individual on such a board has no legal standing. Because it is a corporate body, it must act as a committee of the whole. In dealing with any issue, board members should have the opportunity to participate in a discussion, but in the end, the action of the majority prevails. Once a resolution has been adopted, it is the responsibility of the chief school officer to carry it out.

How does a superintendent maintain a cordial and workable relationship with the members of the board of education? New superintendents will most likely have spent at least some time with the board as a group and perhaps even met with some of them individually. Just as one should quickly get to know as many of the faculty and staff as possible, it is helpful to make every effort to know and learn about the members of the board. One excellent source of information is the other administrators in the district. Of course, their view is only one possible perspective. The previous superintendents or perhaps the interim superintendent can also be helpful. Even though some negative reports about individual board members may circulate, it is essential that a chief school officer establish with them a cordial relationship based on mutual respect.

It is a good idea to begin communications with board of education candidates as soon as they complete their petitions. An informal initial contact by the superintendent might well begin the relationship in a positive way. Once new board members are elected, the superintendent should conduct a personal orientation for each new member. These meetings should include discussions of the board of education policy manual, employee contracts, and minutes of recent meetings. New members should be introduced to the mission statement and current district objectives. During the course of this orientation, it is essential to emphasize the specific roles of the board and the superintendent. Finally, it is important that a superintendent include an explanation of the law in the state regarding open meetings and executive sessions. Board members should know that personal and financial questions are best discussed in executive sessions.

This type of preparation can avoid uncomfortable moments at the first meetings of the new board members. Often state and county school board organizations provide training sessions for newly elected school board members. The superintendent should encourage attendance at these sessions. In fact, it is important that a continuous effort be made to allow board members to attend conferences and meetings at which they can learn more about current educational issues.

If a superintendent is fortunate enough to have an effective board president, it might be helpful to invite him or her to attend the orientation sessions for new board members. It also would be appropriate to ask the newly elected members to attend any sessions of the board that take place prior to their formally taking office.

Of all the issues that can cause problems in a district, the question of the appropriate roles of the board of education and the superintendent is perhaps the most volatile. If all parties can reach such an understanding, it is going to help a district to function more effectively. This objective is easier to identify than it is to implement. Almost everyone knows intellectually that it is the board's job to establish policy and the task of the superintendent to administer the district. Having said this, it is also true that the line between policymaking and administration is not always easily discernable. Hopefully during the interview process, this topic was at least discussed. In any case, the following simple rules should be established:

1. If a citizen or staff member raises a question with a board member, the board member should be requested to suggest that the questioner call the superintendent directly. The other alternative would be to have the board member raise the issue with the superintendent. A return call to the questioner can be made either by the superintendent or the board member. Board members should be asked to say as little as possible to the individual who contacts them until the superintendent has the opportunity to investigate the issue.
2. No one should have to deal with surprises at public board meetings. The superintendent should pledge to give members ample supporting material on the items on the agenda. Board members should also have the opportunity to submit items to be part of the formal agenda. This being done and the agenda published, only emergency items should be added thereafter. Neither the board members nor the superintendent should be required to respond publicly to an item without having the opportunity to prepare. Even when the public is allowed to speak and unscheduled issues are raised, it is not inappropriate to put off a formal response. Of course, if an unscheduled item deals with a personnel question, it should be first discussed in executive session.

Another issue that any board and superintendent must consider is which district employees should be present at board of education meetings. Certainly assistant superintendents and business officials should be in attendance. In smaller districts, building principals might well be asked to be present. A superintendent must be very sensitive to the fact that especially building principals have many other job related evening activities. They, too, need to have the opportunity to maintain a personal life away from school. Other individual faculty and staff members should be invited for agenda items on which they can offer special expertise.

An administrative meeting prior to each board meeting is helpful at which every item on the board agenda is discussed. It is important that the administration offer a united front at board meetings. Any differences need to be settled at the administrative meeting. Although the superintendent should orchestrate board meetings and be the primary educational leader, other district personnel should be given prominent roles in reporting to the board. These individuals should be given adequate time to prepare, and the reports that they will make should be discussed prior to the meeting. A superintendent who tries to do a solo act at every board meeting is more prone to overexposure and errors. The school administration should be seen as a team under the leadership of the superintendent. It is important to ensure that the administrative team is able to do its job without inappropriate interference from board members. It will be difficult to change the habits of a board that is inherited by a new superintendent, but if they can be persuaded to follow the suggestions noted earlier, a number of problems may be avoided.

To ensure that the board functions effectively, the superintendent should also seek to develop the best possible working relationship with the board president. This person can be extremely helpful if an individual board member is causing a problem for the superintendent or other board members. A strong president can deal with such issues. An ideal relationship with a board president would be one characterized by mutual trust and respect. The president should be comfortable discussing with the superintendent any issues; likewise, the chief school officer should feel the same confidence when raising an issue with the leader of the board. On the other hand, it may not be wise to create a relationship that has the superintendent communicating with the president too often. A young superintendent once called the board president on a weather-related decision. He was informed that it was "his call" and that, after all, this is why "we are paying you the big bucks." The president should not be burdened with administrative decisions, but neither should he or she second-guess the superintendent. The goal should be to establish a relationship in which the president shares his or her feelings with the superintendent privately. Of course, it is essential that the president, as well as other board members should not be surprised by news emanating from the school. If a school has a problem and it is likely to become public knowledge, board members need to hear the superintendent's explanation before they read about the issue in the newspaper.

Perhaps the most important aspect of the relationship between the superintendent and the board of education members is that it be even-handed. The superintendent cannot be seen as one who plays favorites. It is essential that he or she remain neutral in board elections and when the board elects officers. With the exception of infrequent private discussions with the president, communications should be shared with all board members. If a Christmas card is sent to one member, other members of the group should also receive them. It is not necessary for the superintendent to entertain board members at home, but if it is done, one must be careful not to give the impression of favoring certain members.

Another important aspect of a chief school officer's relationship with the board is the superintendent's evaluation process that is used in the district. The instrument used for this evaluation should be jointly prepared. One question to ask during this process is whether board members perceive the superintendent to be treating all members equally. If the evaluation identifies a problem in this area or any other crucial category, it should be discussed with the entire board. The evaluation policy should be an important source of feedback. In developing this instrument, the superintendent should take the initiative to ensure that the questions result in information that will help the administrator do a better job. It does not hurt to include some areas of personal strength in the evaluation form. Avoid, if possible, a numerical evaluation. Even though some board members might like the objectivity of numbers, the average results are likely to be affected by circumstances beyond the superintendent's control. An overall rating that goes from a 3.4 to a 3.2 in a particular year may have little to do with what a person has accomplished. It could as easily be a result of poor faculty morale brought about by the lack of a contract.

A part of the evaluation should reflect district and personal goals. When the superintendent and the board mutually agree on the goals, the administrator will have the opportunity to affect his or her evaluation positively. In addition, these goals can give focus to the administration. An evaluation instrument that includes both items on personal leadership and the district objectives is often a good combination. In any case, the superintendent needs to be very active in establishing an evaluation process early in one's career in a new district.

The policy on superintendent evaluations is frequently mentioned in the superintendent's contract. Numerous other conditions of employment should also be present in this important document. Although the compensation provisions of any contract are important, a new superintendent should be especially careful with sections dealing with evaluation, contract renewal, and dismissal. The time frames included in the evaluation and contract renewal sections are often critical. Any decision made on contract renewal should be made at a point during the year that allows the superintendent sufficient time to seek a new position. It should also outline as many safeguards as possible to ensure that if difficulties do arise, a mechanism is in place that allows the superintendent to be informed of any weaknesses perceived by the board. An informal midyear evaluation session can be helpful to ward off future problems. In an article entitled

"My Board Is on the Warpath: What Should I Do?" Robert French gives the following advice:

1. Watch for clues. Are your working relations with the board different from when you first began? Strained? Non-directional? Less supportive? Are board members argumentative? Questioning? Demanding? Negative? If you sense things are not going well, they probably aren't. Recognize the signs, explore your options, and move ahead.
2. Update your professional file. This is a must, even when things are going well. Update your letters of recommendation (Usually, anything over five years is of little value.) Keep your résumé ready.
3. Reaffirm your network of search firms, placement office directors, and professional associates. An informal telephone call will alert these individuals to be on the lookout for job opportunities for you. Don't wait until you have terminated to begin these efforts.
4. Maintain your dignity. You will come out a winner.[1]

The contract should also clearly include fringe benefits and a budget allotment for travel and professional growth expenses. If business expenses are not part of the contract, the superintendent should develop an understanding with the board on this matter. Chief school officers should be attending professional meetings and will need to be out of their offices frequently. In developing an employment contract, a superintendent should seek to negotiate one that will be in place for at least three years. The process of renegotiating a contract is a complex one. It is not inappropriate for a superintendent to consult an attorney prior to agreeing on a formal agreement with the board.

The best possible contract will not guarantee an effective relationship between a superintendent and a board of education. To maintain such a relationship, a wise superintendent will keep several factors in mind. Robert Heller, a veteran administrator at the University of Buffalo and longtime consultant to boards of education, has compiled the following list of recommendations for superintendents:

1. Paramount is the requirement of the superintendent to communicate openly and candidly with the board of education, the total school staff, and the community.
2. No surprises! Keep the board president and other board members apprised of events within the school district.
3. Maintain a system of good written communications. Flooding the system with information is far more desirable than too little written communication.

4. Treat all board members in a friendly, professional manner.
5. Keep as a major goal the development of trust with the board. Be a superintendent of unquestioned integrity.
6. Demonstrate to your board that you are in control of yourself and the management of the school district. Establish a sound evaluation process for the educational program and the staff. The staff evaluation system should be designed to improve the performance of your administrators, teachers, and support personnel. Document and establish a paper trail on each employee. Report periodically to the board the results of the evaluation systems.
7. Be a strong leader by being informed, accept and give criticism plus praise when due, set a positive tone for the district, be consistent in your behavior, don't pout when things don't go your way, learn how to say no, and be honest with yourself and others.
8. Work toward keeping all discussions at board meetings at the issue and concept level. Avoid personalizing discussions or debates.
9. Provide your board with alternatives, particularly with difficult decisions. There is usually no one-and-only solution that puts the board in an either-or situation. Too many alternatives are also inappropriate.
10. Be a good listener. Participate freely but bear in mind, the board meeting is theirs, not yours.
11. Be tolerant and open minded, remaining receptive to new ideas.
12. Stand up for what you believe is best for public education. Exert positive leadership when faced with difficult decisions.
13. Think, stand up for, talk about, and fight with all your might for the kids. Keep the learner the focus of the decision-making process. Remember the three most important aspects of the schools—the kids, the kids, and the kids![2]

Of all the relationships a superintendent will develop within the district, his or her work with the board of education will perhaps be the most challenging. The goal must be to develop a relationship that emphasizes the superintendent and board as a team. Any board needs to see the superintendent as the professional educational leader of the district. One not only must play this role but should seek to be an individual who has earned the respect of the community. A superintendent cannot afford to be perceived as merely another "slick politician." It is important that any educational leader be a mature voice of reason who is primarily concerned with what is best for children. With the high level of distrust of public officials in our society, this will be no easy task, but it must be the ultimate goal.

NOTES

1. French, Robert, "My Board Is on the Warpath: What Should I Do?" AASA Online, <http://www.aasa.org/Issues/CareerAdv/career6.htm> (2000).

2. Fritz Hess, *Guidebook for School Administrators* (East Syracuse: New York State Council of School Superintendents, 1985).

CHAPTER EIGHT

The Superintendent's Relationship with Faculty and Staff Members

Along with the need to create a positive rapport with the board of education, the superintendent must also be very concerned about the faculty and staff in the school district. The impact of administration on faculty and staff morale and job satisfaction has been documented in many studies. Anyone who has ever visited a faculty room knows that school administrators are often the topic of conversation. Too often, the sentiments expressed are negative. Books and articles on teacher burnout often identify administrators' actions as a major cause. Several types of administrative behavior contribute to the unhappiness of faculty and staff.

One problem that is often cited is the failure of administrators to support their employees. Whether it be dealing with problems involving students, parents, or the community, teachers and staff members hope for and often expect their administrators to be a source of support. An administrator at any level who develops a reputation for not being supportive of teachers facing difficult situations is not likely to earn the respect of faculty members. There are times when teachers are wrong, but administrators should still avoid reprimanding or belittling them in the presence of students or parents. When it is necessary to talk about errors in judgment or employee behavior, it should be done in private. A school administrator also should not allow a student or anyone else to be disrespectful to a teacher or staff member during a conference or at a meeting. Especially at public board of education meetings, the superintendent should stop any personal attacks against an employee of the district.

On a positive note, a superintendent must always be seeking ways to offer faculty and staff members commendations for jobs well done. A math teacher in North Carolina said, "I don't think teacher burnout is caused by children. Usually it is the administration. No one strokes you enough."[1] It has often been said that teaching is a very lonely job, and many who have spent years in the classroom can develop the feeling that no one cares about his or her work. They also must hear from their friends and neighbors about the short hours of the school day and the limited number of days students are actually in class. As a superintendent, it is important to constantly seek ways to make faculty and staff members feel appreciated, including publicly acknowledging the many extra hours and days that are part of the teacher's real schedule. One can only be effective in showing appreciation by being visible within the schools and by making a concerted effort to identify the good things that are happening. Personal notes from the superintendent on an accomplishment of a faculty or staff member should be frequent. Telephone calls or e-mails can also be used. When a letter or e-mail communication is sent, note on the bottom that a copy will be filed in the employee's personnel file.

A second criticism of administrators is the lack of respect shown to teachers. There is also the matter of the "sanctity" of the teacher's classroom. Albert Shanker used to tell the story of a high school teacher who "in the middle of one of his most difficult classes had a gorilla suddenly burst into the classroom. Of course, it actually was a student in a costume advertising an upcoming school show. But the interruption turned the class into a shambles. When the teacher complained, he was told that some spontaneity was needed to jazz up the school day." Shanker went on to say that effective administrators know that "their first job is to keep gorillas out of the classrooms."[2]

In most schools, teachers complain about administrative use of the public address system to interrupt classes. Serious teachers care deeply about the limited time they have to teach their lessons, and administrators need to respect their desire not to have frivolous interruptions during the school day.

Another frustrating issue for many teachers is what they see as arbitrary and capricious decisions made by school administrators. During the past forty years, teachers have become increasingly involved in the decision-making process in schools. Still, in some districts teachers and staff members are frustrated by administrators who make professional decisions affecting a teacher's work with little or no consultation. One of the more sensitive issues is when a superintendent is planning a new building or renovations to an existing facility. Art and science teachers expect to play a significant role in the design of new facilities.

Administrators also have to be careful of how their school district deals with complaints about instructional materials. English teachers, health teachers, and librarians believe that their professional expertise should be utilized prior to reacting to parental complaints. Although teachers wish to be involved in decision making, there is a danger of administrators having too many committees. Some teachers thrive on committee work, but many do not. This is especially true if the meetings take the little free time during the school day that teachers have to plan and grade papers. Superintendents need to be careful that teachers are not overburdened with committee work and that certain teachers do not begin to put this professional responsibility ahead of their work in the classroom. It is also true that faculty committees must be seen as being meaningful to teachers. Every committee must have a clear function and meetings must be well organized. The superintendent and the board of education, once they complete their work, must take the reports of these groups seriously. Once a committee has been established, it must be in continual communication with the administrators who formed it. Unless faculty members see involvement on committees as worthwhile, such assignments will just add to teacher frustration.

Paperwork is another cause of teacher dissatisfaction. Devising lesson plans, evaluating student work, maintaining a grade book, preparing report cards, and keeping student attendance records are generally accepted as part of a teacher's job. Most also do not object to preparing an annual budget. Increasingly, classrooms report that there has been a major increase in "busy work." New efforts at assessment and record keeping and participating in the preparation of Individualized Education Programs are among the factors being cited. Administrators must be vigilant when considering additional paperwork for teachers to do, always asking whether that form or report is really necessary. If it is, ways should be found to make it as easy to complete as possible.

In just the last several years, administrative responses to school security and student discipline have become more closely scrutinized. An administration that is perceived by faculty and staff to be insufficiently concerned about creating a safe and secure atmosphere in the district's schools will not receive high marks from employees. A superintendent must convince the entire school community that these issues are district priorities. It is essential that the chief school officer react strongly to school violence, bomb scares, false alarms, and physical or verbal attacks on faculty or staff. When an incident does occur, the superintendent should not be seen as someone who wishes to merely hide the event from the public but rather make it clear to all that such behavior is unacceptable.

In too many schools, teachers "see administrators in an adversarial role, as upholders of bureaucratic rules and regulations that undermine teachers' authority and effectiveness; as having no useful feedback to provide; as not being either supportive, inspiring, or appropriately 'challenging.'"[3] As the leader of the district, it is important to take seriously the responsibility of creating a positive environment. Although it might be an impossible model, one way to think of those who work for the school is to consider them the "school family." Obviously, a group of employees can never reach the same level of intimacy, commitment, and loyalty as a family, but such a group can achieve a common identity and purpose. They also can learn to care about their fellow workers. Finally, people can develop a sense of loyalty to the organization. The superintendent has the primary responsibility of helping faculty and staff focus on the mission of the school. This mission should be centered on a firm commitment to help all children. As the chief school officer, one must not only articulate the vision of what the school should be but also model appropriate behavior.

As the leader of the district, a chief school officer should always demonstrate concern for all of the district employees. The superintendent needs to become acquainted with as many of his or her fellow employees as possible. The school district should in some way acknowledge and celebrate with employees when a new child is born and pay respects when there are deaths in the family. Such gestures by the leader of the school are meaningful for many families.

One way to become acquainted with fellow employees is to socialize during the lunch period. Rather than a superintendent eating alone at his or her desk or going to a restaurant, joining others in the school cafeteria is a good way to be visible and learn. It is not a good idea, especially in small districts, to be seen during the school day often in local restaurants.

Another word of caution should be offered in regard to socializing with individual members of the faculty and staff outside of the school day. Just as with board members, a superintendent's special friendships with faculty members or nonteaching employees will be noticed. Life will be simpler if superintendents develop their close personal friendships with people not so closely connected with their own school district.

Even though the superintendent's relationship with employees may be quite formal, the leader of the district still needs to find ways to create positive group morale. An excellent method for bringing people together is through establishing effective means of communication within the district. A good way to keep people informed is a publication of a weekly bulletin from the superintendent's office. It can be sent to board members, faculty, and all nonteaching staff. On two or three pages each week, the following information can be included:

1. A calendar of all meetings and programs for the coming week (The principals and other supervisors would send me their information.)
2. Coming events in future weeks
3. Successes during the previous week
4. Announcements from faculty and staff
5. Highlights of board of education meetings
6. Births
7. Condolences for deaths in families
8. Birthdays for the coming month (published the last week of the month)
9. Announcements introducing new personnel, changes in responsibility, and position vacancies
10. An appropriate quotation for the week

After a system is in place, preparing such a weekly bulletin is not time-consuming, and it does keep everyone informed. It is also an effective way of giving public recognition to someone who has done a good job.

Another opportunity for bringing employees together occurs whenever the superintendent addresses a large group. Perhaps the best opportunity to share with employees is a districtwide meeting on the day before school opens. These occasions can be used to set a positive tone for the year ahead. It is also a time when recognition can be given to individuals for years of service to the district.

Employee family picnics and holiday parties also help create a sense of unity within the group. A school or district sunshine committee, which uses employee contributions to send gifts or flowers to employees in the hospital or at the time of a family death, is another way of demonstrating to people that they are part of a caring organization.

The model of school employees as a family is far from perfect. Unlike in a family, sometimes a superintendent must make very difficult personnel decisions. Perhaps the most difficult task is dismissing an employee. With an effective supervision program, dismissals will not happen often, but when they do, the superintendent must not avoid this unpleasant aspect of the job. In many cases, the best strategy to follow is to encourage an individual who does not fit well into the organization to resign. In such situations, the administrator should seek to allow the terminated employee to leave the office with self-respect intact, perhaps suggesting that the person could succeed in another place or at another grade level. Still, there is no denying that part of the job is to supervise and if necessary take disciplinary action with employees.

For some, especially superintendents in a larger district, thinking of fellow employees as a "district family" might not be helpful. Another way to envision the district is as a team. Everyone on the team has a role to play in achieving the common goal. Like a basketball coach explaining his role to a "bench warmer," employees must be told often that their role is necessary and important to the organization. It does not hurt for a superintendent to grab a broom and be part of cleanup committees. The superintendent should be seen as someone who is not above rolling up his or her sleeves and helping out.

It is also essential that employees believe that the chief executive of the school will support them when a problem arises with the public. Superintendents should take the responsibility when something goes wrong and not attempt to place the blame on a faculty or staff member. Employees in any organization appreciate their supervisor's willingness to accept responsibility for a problem, even if it is undeserved.

Whether school employees are thought of as a team or as a family, it is the leader's job to encourage everyone toward achieving the common goal of excellence and developing a sincere concern for all children. In doing so, superintendents must promote effective communication and work constantly to create a positive caring relationship among people employed by the district.

Accomplishing these objectives will not be made easier by the presence of employee bargaining units or unions. Because these groups often have interests that are not always the same as the district management, a negative relationship can easily evolve. This is especially true during a period of intense contract negotiations. The superintendent should attempt, whenever possible, to avoid destructive conflict between the district and its employee bargaining units. One must constantly remember that often the goals of the two groups are the same and that cooperation is better than conflict. For instance, it is possible to work with teacher bargaining units on programs such as staff development. Having a committee appointed by the union to work with the administration on superintendent's conference days and other staff development initiatives can help garner support for these programs. Districts have been successful working together with the union in establishing mentor teacher programs. Staff recognition programs can be jointly planned.

A key aspect of successful labor relations is to establish ongoing communication between the union and the administration. If an atmosphere of openness is present, many potential problems can be avoided. It is necessary to include a word of caution regarding the superintendent's relationship with union leaders. One cannot allow this relationship to undercut the work of other members of the management team. Principals and other administrators must be informed and kept involved in any discussions that might affect their responsibilities.

Another matter of concern is the board of education's attitude toward employee bargaining units. Although the superintendent is often tempted to use unions as a scapegoat with the board, in the long run such tactics will be counterproductive. A more positive approach is for the superintendent to help the board understand the rationale for the union's position and to seek ways to resolve potential conflicts. To allow the board to become hostile to its own employees will create a situation of divisiveness within the district. When this happens, the superintendent will eventually be viewed by other employees as the "mouthpiece" for a hostile and insensitive board.

Maintaining a cordial relationship with employee unions is especially difficult during contract negotiations. A superintendent can play several roles during negotiations with employee groups:

1. The superintendent can be the chief spokesperson for the district and take the lead in negotiations.
2. The superintendent can be a member of the team at the table but allow another individual to be the chief spokesperson.
3. The superintendent can remain in the background and not sit at the table during the talks.

The role that an administrator will play varies depending on the conditions in the district. The superintendent's level of expertise and the expectations of the board of education will also affect it.

If a chief school officer is considering taking on the position of the chief spokesperson, several factors should be taken into account. When the superintendent is personally on the "firing line," it is important to know ahead of time whether there is a chance to succeed in a reasonable amount of time and without a great deal of conflict. To do so, it is important to know what the board is likely to accept in a settlement. Before deciding to assume a major role, it would be helpful to have preliminary conversations with those representing the union to provide the opportunity to assess the prospects. If the chances appear good a relatively quick and happy settlement can be reached, a superintendent can enhance his or her image as an effective leader. While a short and successful negotiation will be considered a positive achievement for a superintendent, long and bitter talks can only hurt a superintendent's position with employee groups.

It is possible that the greatest success rate might be when the union is represented at the table by its own members rather than by an outside spokesperson. It is often true that it is simpler to reach a quick agreement with nonteaching units than with a faculty union. The decision of a superintendent to become the spokesperson during contract talks should not be taken lightly, as there is often much to lose. In any case, another district representative should also be a member of the team. Not every superintendent is comfortable in the role of a labor negotiator, and a new superintendent should be very careful in taking on this added responsibility, especially if long and difficult talks are likely.

The second possibility is for a superintendent to be at the table but not act as the chief spokesperson. One should be cautious about playing this role. Being a passive observer may seem to minimize a chief school officer's role as the leader of the organization.

Perhaps a better way is for the superintendent to be chairperson of the negotiations planning committee that prepares the positions and strategy of the team. The spokesperson would then be charged with implementation of the plan. It is often helpful to have a board member as part of the committee or team. In any case, the board of education must give prior approval to the district positions in all negotiations and must be kept informed on the progress of the meetings. It is essential that board members be carefully instructed on the confidentiality of all negotiations. If not at the table, the superintendent must be available to the negotiation team especially during crucial meetings. The superintendent can be in the building and participate in caucuses or be available by telephone. The great advantage of not being directly involved at the table is that it places an administrator in a better position to remain above the struggle and to help craft a final settlement when the time is right. In addition, it is better for a chief negotiator other than the superintendent to be the target of employees' anger and frustration.

Whatever the specific role of the superintendent, it is important that the chief school officer always attempt to focus on what is best for the school and children of the district. As a leader of the faculty and staff, one cannot be perceived as only an apologist for the board; at the same time, the chief school officer should not be thought of by the board and the community as one who wants peace at any price.

Before leaving the question of the superintendent's role with employee bargaining units, it might be helpful to address briefly the issue of grievances. In most employee agreements, grievances are defined as a violation of the contract. When the possibility of grievance first comes to the administration's attention, the primary question is whether the district is violating the contract. If there is a question, seeking a legal opinion may in the long run save money and problems. Sometimes the legal staff of the state's school boards association can give to a district an advisory opinion. If this is not possible, the administration should find a local attorney who specializes in labor relations. Should the attorney suggest that the district is in the wrong, attempt to settle the grievance quickly and informally. If, on the other hand, there does not seem to be a violation of the contract, it is wise to spend the money to have legal counsel throughout the process. Most grievances can be dealt with in the early stages, but if arbitration is necessary, it is best to do everything possible to gain a favorable decision. Generally when the relationship between employee groups and the district is positive, grievance problems are minimal.

Grievances are just one type of problem that can sour the relationship between the district and their employee unions. Whether it is a grievance or a budget dispute, when the board of education and employee groups begin to view each other as the enemy, the byproducts will be distrust and a lack of cooperation. In the end, everyone, including the children, will be hurt.

Like the relationship between the superintendent and the board of education, the superintendent's ability to work with and lead the faculty and staff is an essential ingredient of a successful administration. Failure with either of these groups can cause a new superintendent to be like the administrator who came to his new job in September "fired with enthusiasm" and left in June the same way, "fired with enthusiasm."

NOTES

1. Barry A. Farber, *Crisis in Education: Stress and Burnout in American Teachers* (San Francisco: Jossey-Bass, 1991), 219.
2. Farber, *Crisis in Education,* 220.
3. Farber, *Crisis in Education,* 55.

CHAPTER NINE

Working with the Administrative Team

Faculty and staff members are important, but the individuals a superintendent will work most closely with on a daily basis are the other administrators in the district. Developing an effective working relationship with these individuals will be important in helping any superintendent to succeed. Unless the chief school officer has been promoted from within the organization, the central office administrators and building principals are people who any new superintendent should get to know very early in his or her tenure in the district. Even if the new chief school officer has been in the district for many years, it is important to have a private conversation with each administrator during one's first weeks on the job. If the district is too large and such contacts are difficult, it is still necessary to at least meet with the key administrators in a district.

One might consider going to the administrators' offices rather than summoning them to the central office. Administrators are often more comfortable meeting in their own settings, and with principals, it will allow the new superintendent the opportunity to tour the schools. As suggested earlier, these initial contacts should be primarily a time for listening and learning.

It is especially helpful to develop early on a good rapport with the building principals. Their importance to schools cannot be overemphasized. The Effective Schools Research done during the 1960s and early 1970s identified six major characteristics of successful schools. One of those factors was strong leadership. "Research has shown that students make significant achievement gains in schools where principals:

- Articulate a clear school mission.
- Are a visible presence in classrooms and hallways.
- Hold high expectations for teachers and students.
- Spend a major portion of the day working with teachers to improve instruction.

73

- Are actively involved in diagnosing instructional problems.
- Create a positive school environment.[1]

Of all of the tasks performed by the superintendent of schools, selecting and working with building principals may be among the most important. A chief school officer must always be mindful of the difficulty of the principal's job. They are forced to make many difficult decisions each day. A recent story described in a local paper tells of an elementary principal who did not evacuate the school building immediately on being informed of a possible gas leak in the building. The principal's hesitation in making this decision created enough of a community reaction that she chose to resign her position.[2] Hers was a serious mistake, but principals will make questionable decisions occasionally. Like members of the faculty, they will expect the support of the superintendent when they find themselves in a difficult situation. Superintendents will often find themselves acting as mediators and possibly as arbitrators in conflicts between teachers and other administrators. As the chief school officer, one will have complaints from the representatives of the teacher's union against building principals. Whatever the nature of the problem, it is important to demonstrate some empathy for the administrator. Still, immoral, unethical, or illegal behavior by an administrator cannot be overlooked. In any situation, the superintendent should not undermine fellow administrators by talking about them with others. It is important to respect an administrator's integrity and credibility in the district.

In some cases, there will be administrators whose performances are not acceptable. If this is the case, a planned program of performance improvement would need to be devised. To bring about the desired professional growth, a superintendent might consider the following suggestions:

1. Strongly recommend that the administrator participate in appropriate staff development offerings. If the problem is school discipline, it might be suggested that the administrator attend an appropriate conference or read a book dealing with the issue. Should the weakness be ineffective teacher supervision, specialized conferences and training programs can help someone improve their skills.
2. Make certain that principals have adequate clerical support; if the school is large enough, they should have one or more assistants.
3. An informal mentor program can be put in place that would assign an experienced administrator to work with a struggling principal.

4. Make clear to the building principals what is expected of them. Using district goals and objectives as part of the evaluation instrument will help focus the administrator on the issues that are truly important.

If, despite the efforts of the superintendent, the administrator is still not meeting the expectations of the position, it will be necessary to document specific concerns and the efforts made to help the individual. When it is clear that the district would be better off without an employee and reasonable efforts have been made to help the person improve his or her performance, it should be suggested that it might be best if he or she resigns. In seeking someone's voluntary resignation, the superintendent should always attempt to allow the individual to retain self-respect.

Short of forcing a resignation or terminating someone, there is always the option of some sort of reorganization of the administrative hierarchy. Such plans should not be introduced too soon after a superintendent begins in a new position. It will take time to learn what everyone's role is within an organization. It is also probably not a good idea to do a major reorganization merely to move one person out of a position. A superintendent must be especially careful about adding new administrative positions unless it is absolutely necessary. It goes without saying that many faculty and community members feel that we already have too many administrators and that every new administrator reduces the amount of money available for more pressing educational expenditures. We need to remember that during the past fifteen or twenty years the pattern in businesses in the United States has been to reduce the number of middle managers. Board members are apt to be working in industries where this has been happening. As a result, they may well be skeptical about any increases in middle management. Of course, it can be pointed out to them that compared to most businesses schools have fewer managers. In elementary and secondary schools, the number of persons employed per executive, administrator, and/or manager can be compared using the following ratios: Elementary and secondary schools have a ratio of one manager to approximately fourteen and one half employees. The closest field with such a ratio is transportation, where the ratio is one to nine. In printing and publishing, mining, communications, and public administration, there are fewer than six employees for each manager. The average in all manufacturing is one to seven.[3]

Even with these comparisons, a superintendent will need to be cautious; it is best to wait at least a year before deciding to add new administrative positions. A good time to consider reorganization would be when an administrator retires or leaves the district. Despite the superintendent's efforts to be persuasive on the need for administrative help, in many communities the negative feelings about "overpaid school administrators" will persist. As a result, it is not unusual for principals and other managers in the school district to feel unappreciated. Many people will second-guess their decisions. Often, every option available to them in dealing with a problem will create dissatisfaction in some segment of the school community.

Because they are unlikely to receive frequent praise from other sources, superintendents must give commendations to administrators often for the good work that they do. In producing school district newsletters or issuing press releases, it is important to give appropriate credit to deserving administrators. Where pictures are used in the publication, the administrators should be included. Too many superintendents are so concerned about their own image that they forget about the people who deserve the recognition. How many times do we see a college publication or a school newsletter that contains numerous pictures of the college president or a school superintendent? These publications can be compared to a congressman or senator whose picture appears on almost every page of mailings to constituents. An effective leader does not need to take credit publicly for everything that is positive within the organization but instead uses this recognition as a type of reward for good work.

The same unselfish approach should be taken when reporting to the board of education. Administrators who have had successes should be recognized publicly at board meetings. Just as with other employees, administrators also deserve written commendations from the superintendent. Such positive feedback will undoubtedly encourage future initiatives by the leaders in the district. It cannot be doubted that the superintendent's own success in carrying out of the district objectives will in large part depend on the commitment and enthusiasm of the entire administrative team.

An important aspect of the chief school officer's job is to communicate frequently and clearly his or her own aspirations for the district. When this is done with any group, the sessions should be well planned. Although the chief school officer should prepare the agenda for administrative meetings, all administrators should be encouraged to suggest agenda topics. As a minimum, administrative meetings should be scheduled prior to a board of education meeting. Part of the agenda can be devoted to preparing for the board meeting. All major board agenda items should be discussed. On controversial questions, the entire administrative team should help formulate the administrative position. This being done, the superintendent should make it clear that at the public session unanimity will prevail among the team. Public squabbling among administrators must be avoided. If a consensus cannot be reached at the administrative meeting, the superintendent must formulate the administrative position for the meeting.

Because today many middle-level administrators are members of a union, there might well be issues that create a potential conflict between the superintendent and the administrative bargaining unit. If the middle-level managers are part of a union, they will have negotiated a formal contract with the district. These contracts will include provisions on many areas affecting the terms and conditions of employment. A superintendent must be careful not to ignore the provisions of these contracts. If an administrative grievance is filed, every effort should be made to resolve the problem during the informal stages of the procedure. A chief school officer who frequently becomes embroiled in conflicts with the administrative bargaining unit is going to be less than effective in leading a successful administrative team. This does not mean that the superintendent should allow the administrative union or any other union to run the district through intimidation. After consulting with the school attorney, the superintendent may well realize that grievances need to be contested. Still, one must choose the battles that are worth fighting carefully. Causing antagonism with district administrators over a minor issue can be counterproductive.

Along with the emergence of administrative unions has come a major commitment to the concept of "site-based management." Increasingly individual schools are being given more and more power in decision making. This increased autonomy for principals and their faculties has raised new questions about how best to divide authority between the central administration and the individual school administration. Because more than ever the principal and the teachers of a school are being held accountable for student success, it seems only fair that they participate in decisions on how best to meet the district objectives. Even as schools move in the direction, superintendents must always remember that they will be held ultimately responsible for the new "high-stakes" examination programs that have been imposed in many states. In the new division of power, one area where individual schools are being given additional authority is in budgeting.

Most often the superintendent, with the advice and consent of the board of education, allocates the amounts that can be spent in each category on the budget. Thus, the decision on the exact amount to be expended in transportation, maintenance, and instruction should be determined at the district level. If there is a budget committee made up of community or board members, they, too, can be involved in the general allocation decisions. Once an amount has been assigned to a principal or other superintendent, these individuals and their colleagues should be given considerable latitude. The choice of whether to buy new microscopes for the biology lab or a new set of American history textbooks can be made at the building level. Maintenance supervisors should decide on the amount to be spent on new brooms and lightbulbs. Still, even when this autonomy is granted, the superintendent and his or her staff should monitor proposed expenditures to ensure that enough money is being set aside to meet district objectives.

Although individual schools and departments may have the primary responsibility for specific budget lines, personnel decisions within the district must not be completely delegated. New positions certainly should not be added to the payroll without the superintendent's approval. In fact, the superintendent should maintain the right to approve or disapprove of any personnel recommendations to the board of education. In many states, it is the legal responsibility of the superintendent to make these recommendations. A possible procedure for a chief school officer in a smaller district is to ask the principal and his or her faculty to nominate two or three finalists for each position. The screening process in most districts today is done at the building level by the principal, committee, or teachers; in some communities, members are involved. Once the finalists are determined, the superintendent can interview each candidate. The final step of the process in smaller districts could then be a conversation between the superintendent and the principal or other supervisor to choose the successful candidate. On those few occasions when there is not agreement, perhaps the best way to proceed is to continue the search.

A large district will present too many personnel decisions for the superintendent to carry on interviews with numerous candidates. Even with a heavy schedule, however, the superintendent should find time to become very involved in the selection of individuals to fill leadership positions. Principals are so important in any school that a superintendent would be making a mistake not to participate in these crucial personnel decisions.

One type of candidate recommendation that can cause superintendents a problem is a person who is a resident of the community or a friend of a board member. It even can be difficult if the person is close to another administrator in the district. With such applications, it is helpful if there is a committee at the building level to help screen applicants. A chief school officer who becomes heavy handed in either promoting or vetoing a local candidate can become embroiled in a very unpleasant situation. To help avoid such conflicts, a district policy prohibiting or at least somehow regulating the employment of close relatives of board members, administrators, or faculty members is useful. It is especially important that superintendents do not open themselves up to charges of nepotism.

Administrators should not hire their own relatives, especially in a community with a high unemployment rate. An argument can be made for giving local residents priority. Since these people are likely to be property tax payers in the district, there might well be a strong sentiment toward choosing local people. On the other hand, it is essential to avoid the feeling in the district that getting hired depends on who a person knows. One of the values of a civil service system covering nonteaching personnel is that it can make it easier for school administrators to avoid hiring less qualified candidates who happen to be well connected within the district.

The choices made in hiring new personnel are perhaps the most important decisions made by a school administrator. A superintendent must be a major player in this process so that favoritism and local politics do not create issues within the district. Of course, in the choice of administrators, superintendents should maintain the right to make the final recommendations. Since the chief school officer will be working closely with and depending on these individuals, it is absolutely necessary that these positions be filled with the best people available. Recruitment needs to be done carefully, and the superintendent should be willing to advertise regionally or nationally. An important aspect of the selection process should be the checking of references. Superintendents should take the time to ask the right questions about administrative candidates they are considering.

A third area where delegation can occur is in the purchase of instructional materials and other supplies. Department heads and principals should be given sufficient latitude in this area. Even here, the superintendent must exercise leadership to ensure that adequate funds are allotted to aid in the implementation of the district's objectives. In this regard, the superintendent must also monitor the overall curriculum offerings of the school district. This is especially true in a larger community with a number of schools. Any size district needs someone who will ensure that there is an organized plan in every area of the curriculum and that district instructional objectives are emphasized in the plan. Complete curricular autonomy for individual schools in a district can lead to unnecessary repetition and serious academic gaps in a student's education. A well-thought-out K–12 curriculum must be in place in every subject. The secondary health teachers must know what is being taught at the elementary level. We cannot have sixth grade teachers in one district school teaching American history as their social studies and another school emphasizing African and Asian studies. If the district is too small to have a central office administrator assigned as the instructional leader, the superintendent must lead and monitor curricular and instructional budget decisions. Someone in the district also needs to ensure that the curriculum mandates of the school are being met. As noted earlier, too often superintendents leave little time to become involved in the actual instruction of children. A superintendent cannot do all of these things without significant assistance from the administrative team. Despite this reliance, there is an equal danger that a chief school officer will abdicate all personnel and budget decisions to others. The goal must be to create a collaborate team that is guided by a superintendent with a clear vision for the future of the district.

A final thought related to the topic of the administrative team is necessary. Perhaps one of the most important individuals in helping the superintendent succeed is the office secretary or administrative assistant. The following are several important qualities to look for in selecting individuals for this position:

1. It is important to note that the receptionist in the superintendent's office creates the first impression with visitors, both in greeting someone entering the office and also in speaking to people on the telephone. Establishing a helpful and hopefully cheerful environment in the superintendent's office is extremely important. We have all visited offices where the staff members' attitudes and behavior have affected our feelings toward the person we were waiting to see. Most of us have also been treated less than politely when telephoning an office. A superintendent's office staff can be businesslike without being intimidating. The person who represents the superintendent in the office influences greatly whether it is a pleasant place to visit.
2. A secretary must be trustworthy. Confidentiality in a superintendent's office is essential. A secretary who gossips can create terrible situations for a superintendent. More than confidentiality, it is helpful to have an assistant who will offer suggestions and look

for ways to improve the office. A secretary who is a shrewd judge of people can also help with personnel decisions. A job candidate who is less than positive with the secretary is probably not someone you would want to hire. It is often helpful if a trusted secretary has had some time with the candidate to ask, "What did you think of Mr. X?"

3. Finally, when selecting a person to be a secretary or an administrative assistant, it is wise to seek someone who might compensate for one's own weaknesses. If the superintendent is a poor speller or has marginal computer skills, it is advisable to seek someone who can help make up for these deficiencies. An administrator who is a poor record keeper needs someone who can maintain the file system for the office. Superintendents who have trouble staying with the schedule might need someone who would be unafraid to prod them.

When beginning a new job, it is likely that the secretary in the office will be loyal to the person who is leaving. For that reason, it is important to take the time to learn about the existing practices in the office and listen carefully to this person's opinions. When it is decided that changes in the office must occur, they should be made in cooperation with the secretary. It is important not to criticize the practices of the former superintendent and to allow sufficient time before making changes. Loyal secretaries can be instrumental in a superintendent's success, or they can become just another personnel problem. Because a superintendent will spend as much time with the office secretary as with any other district employee, it is essential that a trusting relationship evolve. If there seems to be a hint of a problem, do not let it fester, but take the time to work things out. Poor personal chemistry within any office group can create an unpleasant workplace.

Secretaries and administrative staff can become either the greatest allies of a superintendent or the most frequent detractors. These individuals cannot be taken for granted, and any superintendent must continually demonstrate that the work they do is appreciated. It is also important that the chief school officer views these individuals as more than mere employees but rather treat them as valued colleagues. People can tell when a superintendent is simply using them to further personal goals. Such a self-centered leader will never gain the respect and trust of colleagues and thus will have difficulty in motivating people to bring about positive change within the organization.

NOTES

1. Myra Pollack Sadker and David Miller Sadker, *Teachers, Schools and Society* (New York: McGraw-Hill, 1994), 145–46.

2. *Batavia Daily News,* 13 March 2000, i.

3. Gerald W. Bracey, *Setting the Record Straight* (Alexandria, Va.: Association for Supervision and Curriculum Development, 1997), 173.

CHAPTER TEN

The Superintendent as an Instructional Leader

If an appropriate relationship with the administrative team has been developed, it will be much easier to carry out one of the chief roles as the instructional leader of the district. In an era characterized by teacher empowerment and site-based management, the role of the school administrator as an instructional leader is changing. Administrators, particularly the superintendents, are no longer expected to be the sole change agents in the district. Today, change in schools often begins in an individual school or even in a single classroom rather than being imposed by the central office.

Obviously the superintendent's vision and ideas should be a major factor in determining the instructional objectives of the district. This can only be true if others perceive the superintendent as a person who values school improvement initiatives. By creating a positive and encouraging environment for change, superintendents will become the major players in the quest to find better ways to help children learn. Creating such an environment and facilitating instructional growth must be a primary role of the superintendent of schools.

In the book *Staying Centered: Curriculum Leadership in a Turbulent Era*,[1] Steven J. Gross identifies ten qualities of curriculum leaders. Those leaders who are classified as being successful all had the following characteristics:

1. *"Experienced but still growing."* The experiences of successful curriculum leaders most often included work as classroom teachers. In addition, they knew the setting they were working in and they saw themselves as people who were growing and evolving. Although they had considerable experience, they were not tied to the status quo.

2. *"Centered on students and families."* Those curriculum leaders making a positive difference in their districts were focused on student learning. Any innovation was measured by its potential success in helping children and families.

3. *"Willingness to experiment but not reckless."* Often leaders insisted on a tryout period for new ideas. There also was a willingness to take the necessary time required to prepare people for change. Districts planning major changes would not begin in April to change their high school to block scheduling in September.

4. *"Highly engaged but not overwhelmed."* One leader described the goal as "taking the work but not yourself seriously."[2] Despite interruptions and setbacks, the leaders maintained the vision for the group and kept them on track. At the same time, they did not appear fanatical or driven.

5. *"Trusting but not naïve."* Leaders gave trust and thus received it from colleagues. At the same time, they did not harbor unrealistic expectations for others. The leaders understood that those participating in the group attempting to bring about change had other priorities and concerns. As a result, the leaders let the process unfold without pushing too hard.

6. *"Powerful but not overbearing."* The group must feel that they have support from the top but not domination by a dictator.

7. *"Visible but quiet."* The leader must continually show enthusiasm and actively participate in the process, but it is not necessary to be a person who talks more than others. Informal contacts with teachers and students were used to encourage the process.

8. *"Dignified but informed."* As a leader, it is important to strike the appropriate balance between informality and serious purpose. It is essential that leaders be willing to laugh and have fun with the group but at the same time maintain a level of formality that signifies the seriousness of the task.

9. *"Demanding but understanding."* Although patient, leaders expect high levels of performance. If a subcommittee is assigned to explore a certain aspect of the program being considered, the leader must make it clear that the group must do a thorough job on their assignment. If the superintendent is chairing a group, it is important that agendas and minutes are always prepared. Everything about the process should be professional, but if a person or group occasionally falls short, the leader must not embarrass or humiliate group members.

10. *"Highly ambitious but for their group, not themselves."* The leader in curriculum change must do everything possible to help the group feel strongly about the goals being pursued. Teachers should be encouraged to attend conferences and make visitations to other schools. The willingness of leaders to expend district funds on individual members of the team emphasizes the importance each individual has to the project. The goals must be shared, and not just those of the leader.

A district that is truly committed to instructional improvement must also develop a staff development program that is closely aligned with academic objectives and is ongoing. For too long in many districts, staff development has meant two or three conference days a year. These programs were often planned around outside motivational speakers or days that offered a smorgasbord of diversified offerings in an attempt to meet the many varied interests of the faculty. Frequently, there was little or no follow-up to these programs. If the program featured an engaging and humorous speaker or two and a good luncheon, such one-day conferences were often considered successful. In recent years, research and actual experience by districts have demonstrated that targeted and long-term staff development programs do result in instructional improvement.

In a recent edition of *Educational Leadership* highlighting faculty development, Linda Darling-Hammond lists several characteristics of a successful professional development program. She writes that

it is centered around critical activities of teaching and learning—planning lessons, evaluating student work, developing curriculum—rather than abstraction and generalities; it grows from investigation of practice through cases, questions, analysis, and criticism; and it is built on substantial professional discourse that fosters analysis and communication about practice and values in ways that build colleagueship and standards of practice.[3]

A teacher's personal program of professional development begins with their college preparation and must continue for their entire career. Professional development for administrators should also be thought of in the same way. Planning such a program can only be done jointly by teachers and administrators. Another way of describing a high-quality development program was included in the same magazine in an article entitled "Building Learning into the Teaching Job" by Judith Renyi. She cites the National Foundation for the Improvement of Education, which describes a high-quality professional development as having the following characteristics:

1. Has the goal of improving students' learning
2. Helps teachers meet the future needs of students who learn in different ways and who come from diverse backgrounds
3. Provides adequate time for inquiry, reflection, and mentoring and is an important part of the normal working day of all educators
4. Is rigorous, sustained, and adequate to the long-term change of practice
5. Is directed toward teachers' intellectual development and leadership
6. Fosters a deepening of subject-matter knowledge, understanding of learning, and appreciation of students' needs
7. Is designed and directed by teachers, incorporates the best principles of adult learning, and involves shared decisions
8. Balances individual priorities with school and district needs
9. Makes best use of new technologies
10. Is site-based and supports a clear vision for students[4]

Following such guidelines will undoubtedly increase student learning. An important related question is, How can school districts best measure student learning? For many years we have heard critics of our testing procedures talk and write about more authentic assessment measures. In some places, portfolios, skills tests, and oral examinations are supplementing traditional forms of evaluation. Still, with the standards movement, traditional testing appears to be taking on greater significance. Statewide achievement tests are being introduced in a number of states along with national norm reference tests. The increased importance being given to test results will undoubtedly have impact on the superintendency.

In some places, test results have become the primary way that boards of education judge the success of their chief school officer. The February 2000 issue of *Educational Leadership* was devoted to trying to answer the question "What do we mean by results?" Articles describe how to use instructional rubrics to evaluate student work, how to analyze and learn from test results, and how to create "data-driven schools." At the same time, many cautions are expressed about giving too much emphasis to traditional testing. Dale Wallace suggests that "prompting, prepping, and price tags connected to testing do little to improve education."[5] He goes on to say that "provincial achievement exams create undue pressure on students, teachers, and schools. Even worse, the tests fail to assess what students need to know to be citizens of the twenty-first century." The author believes that "[s]tudents deserve better. They deserve to be taught to think."[6]

Criticism of the growing reliance on tests will continue, but in today's climate superintendents cannot ignore the test results of their students. Where weaknesses are obvious, the administrative team must work with appropriate faculty to ensure that a plan is in place to deal with the deficiencies. At the same time, the superintendent must avoid making principals and teachers paranoid over test results. There are some districts in which valuable educational activities have been shortchanged because the district seems to care about little else than test results. Additional drill and practice have replaced field trips and guest speakers. In some cases, subjects other than language arts and math have been severely limited to bring up test scores. A good set of test scores that are shared with the public will often bring academic recognition for the school, while outstanding concerts, art exhibits, and plays go unrecognized. A superintendent who overemphasizes test results can create unnecessary and unproductive stress within the district.

Administrators and faculty members must continually ask how much of what is being tested truly reflects "real learning." It could be that what we are really doing in many cases is testing students' skills in memorizing facts. One must be open to a variety of assessment instruments and not be tyrannized by the current craze for test results. Poor scores can show a deficiency in a program and should lead to studies that will allow an appropriate response, but they should not result in a panic and a reliance on "quick fixes." If it appears that the primary concern of the superintendent is test results, administrators and teachers will probably respond, but as the district's leader, it is important to remember that important educational objectives exist other than improving students' scores.

Whether it is better test results or other equally important instructional objectives, these topics should be an integral part of the agenda at administrative and board of education meetings. It is often helpful at board meetings to invite groups of teachers to report and discuss with the board specific academic programs. Not only is this a time when the faculty and the board can interact, but it can also help establish a feeling of mutual respect. Such dialogues also demonstrate to the professional staff that the district is indeed interested in what is happening in the classrooms. These interactions should be as informal as possible and allow time for discussion. It is a good plan to have the teachers present for refreshments so that there can be social interaction with the board.

Superintendents and board members also have the responsibility to be informed and politically involved in what is occurring at the state and national levels in the area of instruction. Although the current stated thrust in reform is to allow more local autonomy, the resulting changes might well lead to the opposite. As the chief educational authority in the district, the superintendent needs to read educational publications from Washington and the state capital and react and respond to possible initiatives by state and federal governments.

Working as an active member of the state's superintendent organization is one way to have a voice. It is also helpful to communicate with local state legislators. No district should become isolated or provincial in its thinking. Administrators and teachers must conduct themselves as professionals with an obligation to identify and evaluate new ideas. We cannot afford to jump on every educational bandwagon, but neither can we ignore the parade.

Finally, it is important that the chief school officer demonstrate a commitment to academic excellence. Publishing the honor roll, attending honor society inductions, and writing letters to students who have achieved scholastic distinction are just some of the ways to demonstrate that the chief school officer cares about scholastic achievement.

As superintendent, encouraging professional discussion and planning is also critical. Even though common planning periods for teaching team members are difficult to schedule, with proper leadership they can be very beneficial. The district budget also is a way to help implement instructional improvement. In some districts, the staff development budget allotments are the first items cut. The chief school officer may have to decide on occasion to put off the purchase of a new pickup truck for the maintenance department or new band uniforms to ensure that money is available for instructional improvement projects. In any case, the superintendent's attitude toward instruction will strongly impact the district's programs. For that reason, superintendents must constantly remind themselves that what is occurring in the classrooms is the most important factor in determining their own success and that of the children of the district.

NOTES

1. Steven J. Gross, *Staying Centered: Curriculum Leadership in a Turbulent Era* (Alexandria, Va.: Association for Supervision and Curriculum Development, 1998), 11–12.

2. Gross, *Staying Centered,* 6.

3. Linda Darling-Hammond, "Teacher Learning That Supports Student Learning," *Educational Leadership* 5 (February 1998): 6–11.

4. Judith Renyi, "Building Learning into the Teaching Job," *Educational Leadership* 5 (February 1998): 72.

5. Dale Wallace, "Results, Results, Results?" *Educational Leadership* 5 (February 2000): 66–70.

6. Wallace, "Results, Results, Results?" 68.

CHAPTER ELEVEN

The Superintendent and the Law

The job of a superintendent would be easier if the only responsibilities were instructional leadership and personnel. Unfortunately, today's superintendent cannot avoid a number of areas. One of the most complicated and difficult matters is the involvement in school law and government regulations.

Responsibility for the governance of education in the United States under our federal system is divided between the federal and state governments, along with the local school districts. Laws and regulations can be very confusing and sometimes can conflict depending on the level of government. Historically, public education governance has been reserved primarily for state and local governments. During the second half of the twentieth century, the federal government took on a more active role. Although Washington on the average provides only 7 percent of the revenue for schools, increasingly federal laws and court decisions have affected not only school budgets but also the actual programs being offered. The Great Society programs of the mid-1960s gave us Head Start and Title I of the Elementary and Secondary Education Act of 1965. Head Start targeted disadvantaged children and helped bring about the preschool movement, which has grown to the point where a significant percentage of parents at all economic levels are now enrolling their three- and four-year-old children in private and public programs. Title I has provided financial aid to school districts for remedial programs in reading and math. Title IX of the 1972 Educational Amendments protected female students from discrimination, but in the process it has created some interesting problems for school administrators. The many competitive categorical grant programs that have been introduced have created the new specialty of grant writer in many districts.

Perhaps the federal law with the greatest impact has been Public Law 94-142 and the subsequent additions to the laws, especially the Individuals with Disabilities Education Act passed in 1990. Since 1975, when Public Law 94-142 was signed, school districts in the United States have spent billions of dollars to offer special services to the approximately 11 percent of our students who have been classified as children with special needs. This has included children from birth until age twenty-one. Superintendents and boards of education are constantly interacting with their local special education committees, as well as individual parents and groups of parents representing those children involved in special education.

Along with legislation and the federal regulations that implement these laws, schools have been greatly impacted by decisions of the federal judiciary. The 1954 case *Brown v. Board of Education of Topeka, Kansas,* quickly comes to mind. By ruling that racial segregation in our schools was "inherently unequal," a new era in public education was introduced. The problem of racially segregated schools is still with us as we enter into the twenty-first century.

Another area affected by court decisions is the ongoing and ever-changing interpretation of the First Amendment in regard to church and state. The courts are continually redefining the relationship between public schools and parochial schools. Superintendents will sometimes be involved with questions relating to the legal responsibilities of the public school district to provide transportation, textbooks, and special services to their local religious schools. Questions on holiday celebrations, religious music, and Bible studies will face superintendents, especially in those districts with diverse populations. Affirmative action programs can be added to the list of areas being affected by judicial decisions.

Without question the federal government has become a major player in education, which has resulted in placing education in a prominent place in the political arena. The two major political parties have a different view as to how to solve the educational problems of this country. President Clinton and his fellow Democrats supported legislation for additional federal funding to finance extra teachers and to repair school buildings, but they also championed programs for national curriculum standards and testing. Democrats tend to believe that the federal government can help alleviate the problem that Jonathan Kozol has labeled the "savage inequalities" in our nation's schools. There is no question that districts located in affluent suburbs can spend two or three times as much per pupil as schools located in urban and some rural districts. As long as our system remains heavily reliant on local property taxes, it leaves to the state governments the responsibility to use their state aid for education to remedy the inequalities in educational spending. Many Democrats argue that because state governments cannot or will not make the required adjustments, the federal government must do more to ensure equal educational opportunities whether the students are attending a wealthy Long Island school district or a school in rural Mississippi. Of course, both of the national teacher's unions support strongly the Democratic position on education.

On the other hand, most Republicans are not convinced that the role of the federal government in education should be increased. When the Republican Party took control of Congress in 1994, a number of conservative Republicans advocated the abolition of the federal Department of Education. These individuals saw the department as a bloated bureaucracy that wasted taxpayer money and had little positive impact on student achievement. Instead, many Republicans believe that the answer to our educational problems is school choice. Specifically, the party has supported the implementation of a voucher system that would offer parents the financial ability to send their children to public or private schools. This choice would result in a healthy competition that Republicans believe would increase the effectiveness of most schools. Those schools that did not improve would cease to exist. As participants in the public dialogue on education, superintendents must be ready to speak in an informed manner on topics such as federal involvement in education and school choice.

Although the debate will continue over the appropriate federal role in education, state governments continue to be extremely important in the way schools are governed. Some states have more involvement than others, but all state governments are active in passing legislation and regulations that affect curriculum and, now more frequently, assessment. Many states have been active in recent years in strengthening high school graduation requirements and also teaching and administrative certification. Many have passed laws regarding student discipline, transportation, and health and safety standards. Thousand of laws are introduced in state legislatures regarding every phase of education, from teacher tenure to eligibility in interscholastic athletics. These laws lead to hundreds of pages of regulations that are prepared to help implement the intent of the legislation. Decisions of state courts also can impact what happens in schools. In some states, the state commissioner or superintendent of education also has judicial powers.

A superintendent must have some general knowledge of current judicial decisions, along with a basic understanding of laws and regulations promogated by their state government. Many chief school officers also are active politically with their local state legislators. Sometimes a relationship can be built that will encourage legislators actually to initiate communication with superintendents concerning proposed legislation. State organizations of administrators also are an avenue for influencing state government.

Although it is important to be conversant with federal and state laws and court cases, the primary responsibility of the superintendent is to be a leader in the discussion concerning legal and policy matters at the local level. Every district should have a manual containing all policies approved by the board of education. These locally adopted rules govern such areas as personnel practices, financial procedures, and emergency plans. It is the superintendent's responsibility to ensure that these policy handbooks are kept current and periodically reviewed. Contracts with employee groups will also contain provisions that will affect administrative actions and decisions. Any administrator who is ignorant of contract language and district policy can be in danger of creating grievances and other personnel problems. If a policy calling for three formal observations of each nontenured teacher is ignored, a later attempt to dismiss such a teacher could be in jeopardy. A contract clause that states that a teacher who is not going to receive tenure be notified by 1 April must be taken seriously. Local policies on the selection of textbooks and library materials need to be carefully followed to help protect the district when questions are raised concerning the appropriateness of certain magazines or books being used by the school. Ignorance of the contract or the district's policy is not an excuse for violating it. State school board organizations can often be helpful to superintendents in the area of policy development by providing sample wording. In any case, it is the chief school officer's job to propose needed policies. For instance, a district without a well-thought-out plan for emergency evacuation of the buildings or for early dismissals will find itself improvising every time a crisis occurs.

Local policies, state and federal laws and regulations, and court decisions make up a huge and ever-changing body of information that will be important in helping superintendents meet their professional responsibility. Because of this, it is undoubtedly useful for a school administrator to have prior academic training in school law. Any educational administration program should include instruction in this important area. Superintendents should not only be exposed to current political and legislative issues but also be taught how and where to seek information about these topics. Anyone who becomes a superintendent without such academic background should either enroll in a school law course or make it a high personal priority to become informed. Perhaps more than almost any other area, a practicing superintendent must seek to stay current on governance issues at all levels.

No amount of academic preparation or personal study will prepare a superintendent for all of the legal problems that might be experienced. With this in mind, every district should have a source of reliable legal advice available. Counsel should be sought whenever an issue has reached the point where litigation is possible. Boards of education are often not forgiving when a superintendent makes a costly error without seeking appropriate legal advice. It is extremely important to choose attorneys who are knowledgeable in the field of education. Large law firms often have specialists in the field. Information on effective school attorneys can also be sought from veteran superintendents or state administrative or school board organizations. In some cases, state organizations also employ a staff of attorneys who are available to superintendents for advisory opinions at no cost to the district. For minor questions, such sources can save a district money.

Needless to say, legal services can be very expensive. Larger districts may have an attorney as a permanent member of the administrative team. Many other districts will have a lawyer on retainer to attend important meetings and give advisory opinions on legal issues that do not require excessive research or involve litigation. For these more time-consuming services, the district would pay a law firm on an hourly basis. Most smaller districts compensate their attorneys based on billable hours. These hours include travel time for the lawyer, as well as payment for duplication and other office services. For many districts, it is probably cost effective for school administrators to travel to the attorney's office rather than pay $100 an hour for the attorney to drive to and from the school. Also, paying by the hour will include time spent talking with the attorney on the telephone. Even though it might be pleasant to engage in social conversation, it can be costly when paying by the minute. When being billed on an hourly basis, it is sometimes prudent to consider contacting a higher-priced attorney if that person is a specialist in the field. Local lawyers who are generalists can spend a great deal of time researching an issue that the specialist might answer without any time being spent on legal research.

The advantages of specialists are also evident when hiring someone to be the chief spokesperson for the district in contract negotiations. Most teacher unions can and often do have a professional at the table, and that person, even if he or she is not an attorney, will have access to an expert legal staff. Another time when it is wise to seek professional expertise is when the district is involved in a major financial transaction such as selling bonds to finance a construction project. Superintendents will be called on to make recommendations to the board of education when professional consultants are hired by the school district. Some boards wish to become involved in the selection of professional negotiators, financial advisors, insurance agents, architects, and attorneys. Board involvement in such decisions sometimes helps save the superintendent if the professional selected turns out to be unsatisfactory. Even if the board participates, it will be the responsibility of the superintendent along with the administrative team to check references and to ensure that only well-qualified applicants are considered.

Even though the district hires expert professional advisers, it will still be the superintendent who will be responsible for decisions. Often the choice on a legal matter becomes whether to settle the issue out of court or take it to arbitration or to a formal legal proceeding. Too often, especially in liability cases, the insurance companies that are providing a district's legal protection are likely to settle the cases out of court. Even when claims against the district are of dubious merit, it is frequently less expensive for the company to pay a compromised settlement. Of course, such settlements can lead in the future to higher premiums for the school district. They also might encourage others to seek financial redress from the school system.

There are legal situations in which insurance companies are not involved. For instance, when grievances are filed, the administration must weigh the cost of arbitration, the likelihood of gaining a favorable decision, and any precedent that might be created if the district settles or gains an unfavorable decision. A possible outcome of mishandling a grievance could be future challenges from other employees and therefore, additional legal costs in the future. The superintendent should not only consult an attorney but also consider seeking the views of the board of education.

The legal situations that often have the most public and financial impact on the district are ones that involve student accidents. These cases can arise as a result of injuries occurring in athletics, on school buses, or on the playground. Such incidents can also give the district unwanted publicity. Often, quiet out-of-court settlement is best for all parties, especially if the district was indeed negligent.

The problems that school districts experience because of lawsuits cannot be minimized. In an article reprinted in the *Education Digest,* Sherman Joyce cites the following information from research done by the National Association of Secondary Principals and the National Association of Elementary School Principals:

1. Sixty-five percent of the school principals surveyed reported that school-related programs had been affected because of liability concerns and costs. Some programs were actually ended because of these concerns.
2. Seventy-eight principals of the approximately five hundred surveyed ended all physical contact with students due to lawsuits.
3. One-quarter of the principals said that they had been involved in lawsuits or out-of-court settlements during the last two years.

The study also showed clearly that the frequency of legal problems being faced by schools has dramatically increased during the last decade.[1]

After demonstrating the seriousness of the problem, Joyce suggests that schools consider the following actions to avoid the risk of being sued:

1. Administrators should establish a policy that mandates that a school employee "never touch a student unless it is absolutely necessary to protect the safety of the student or others."[2]
2. Administrators should never dismiss without a thorough investigation complaints or even rumors relating to sexual harassment or child abuse.
3. Administrators should keep careful records during any investigation involving students or staff that could potentially lead to legal action. Administrators should study carefully all requirements for field trips. Although they may not be legally binding, districts should gain written authorization from parents or legal guardians for all field trips.
4. Administrators should ensure that all equipment and facilities are in good working order. This point is especially important with playgrounds located on school grounds.
5. Administrators should be certain that adequate supervision is provided for all school-sponsored activities. Administrators should require parents to notify the school of any medical problems or conditions of their children.[3]

A superintendent who does not stress these measures could well spend a good deal of time and district money reacting to avoidable problems. In preparing for the likelihood of liability claims against the district, a new superintendent should investigate the district's liability insurance policies. In doing so, it is important to ascertain whether coverage is offered for all employees and also for the members of the board of education. The board has the need to be protected just as much as faculty and staff members. Along with liability insurance, the superintendent is responsible for making certain that there is adequate coverage for the building, grounds, and all the contents of all buildings. The agents dealing with the district should aid an administrator in maintaining appropriate policies. Although in many districts insurance services are often put out for bid, it is important that the superintendent and the business office create a strong relationship with the insurance professionals who are serving them. Once again, experience in the field of education is helpful.

Districts should evaluate special optional types of policies. For example, coverage is available to pay for student injuries that take place on school grounds. These policies are expensive and often duplicate coverage that many families have on their children. Should a school district decide not to purchase this type of insurance, it could consider making available an optional policy that parents could choose to purchase. Such a policy would be especially valuable for students who are participating in athletics. If the district does not have an accident policy and only carries liability insurance, parents need to be informed. Some districts prepare a sign-off sheet for parents on which they agree to be responsible for the medical expenses that might be incurred while the student is participating in an interscholastic sport.

Superintendents should anticipate the potential problems that can occur when students are injured at school. Some parents will likely attempt to recover medical costs resulting from a school accident. Sometimes it is better for the district to pay these costs rather than be sued for "inadequate supervision" or address some other charge that might lead to legal expenses and possibly a larger settlement. Even if the district carries an accident insurance policy, it is still possible to be sued. The best defense against such problems is to ensure adequate supervision by qualified personnel. Even if the state does not require physical education teachers and coaches to be trained in first aid or CPR, it is a good policy to be adopted at the local level.

Another dangerous practice is to allow several hundred students on the playground during the school day with one staff member supervising them. Sometimes this situation occurs while other teachers and aides are in the building or on a coffee break. Inadequate supervision is a difficult charge to defend in court. It is also necessary to be aware of and publish any state regulations in regard to teacher aides and student teachers — specifically, whether these individuals can be left in the classroom alone to supervise children. Certainly a school is in danger of a lawsuit if classrooms are left unattended and a student is injured. Teachers and staff must continually be made aware that they are legally responsible for the students assigned to them.

Another legal area that is increasingly a problem for schools is the issue of child custody. With broken families, it is not unusual for unauthorized spouses or unmarried partners to come to the school office and ask for the release of a child. Numerous kidnappings have occurred in this way. If possible, office personnel should have an updated record on legal custody for children. Most often the responsible person informs the school as to the legal custody status. In any case, it is important that every school have a system to safeguard themselves from incidents in which unauthorized adults are allowed to take children from the school building. Unfortunately, legal battles between parents over children are frequent, and often school personnel are drawn into these unpleasant situations.

Potential legal problems can also arise when outside groups are allowed to use the grounds or school buildings. Before giving permission to a group to sponsor an activity in a school building or on school grounds, it is necessary to find out whether this group has adequate insurance or whether the school's policy will cover any incident that might lead to legal action. Even if the sponsoring group does have insurance, it is still very possible that, as the owner, the school will be sued.

All of these potential problems require that all school employees be vigilant when a complaint does occur. It is usually the superintendent who will be served with the legal papers. As a result, it will be the chief school officer's responsibility to make certain that the district is defended. The superintendent is not likely to be completely aware of all of the situations that have led to the lawsuit, but once a case begins it is important to follow the developments carefully until the problem is solved. In the long run, the best policy is for a school district to be aggressive in developing the necessary policies and procedures that will avoid legal actions against the school. This is a responsibility that no superintendent can take lightly.

NOTES

1. Sherman Joyce, "Keeping Schools from Being Sued," *Education Digest* 8 (April 2000): 5 (condensed from *High School Magazine*, February 2000).

2. Joyce, "Keeping Schools from Being Sued," 8.

3. Joyce, "Keeping Schools from Being Sued," 8.

CHAPTER TWELVE

Surviving in the Political Arena of the Community

Much more than knowledge of the law is necessary for a superintendent to successfully maintain the support of the residents of a school district. There are many individuals and groups whose interest in school issues will cause them to attempt to influence the superintendent. Particularly active will be organizations such as employee unions, parent teacher associations, and possibly taxpayers' leagues. Other groups will have their own special causes. Booster clubs for the sports and music departments can be very helpful in raising money for their respective programs, but they can also be difficult if for some reason they decide that the varsity basketball coach or band director is incompetent.

Organizations of parents and children with learning disabilities or attention deficit disorder can also be strong advocates in some communities. A small but articulate group is seeking special programs for children who are identified as being gifted. Depending on the issue, the senior citizens of a school district can also become active, especially when a property tax increase is being considered. The same can be true of businesspeople and farmers. Of course, any problem in the district can lead to the formation of an ad hoc group of concerned citizens. A violent incident in school can quickly lead to a group that will lobby for increased security measures.

A superintendent must be prepared to deal with any of these contingencies. First, it is important to be available to people who have concerns. This approach is ineffective, however, unless the administrator is perceived as a good listener. Although chief school officers should listen carefully to people who seek their help, it is important to be cautious when making commitments for immediate action. Often it is more appropriate to suggest that some time is needed to investigate the problem. Sometimes a problem can be dealt with immediately, but most are complicated enough to require further study and thought. When a reasonable and prudent response has been formulated, it is necessary to communicate with the people who have initiated the issue.

While engaged in discussions about school problems, the superintendent's responses should be consistent. One should not say one thing to a representative of the taxpayers' league and another to the president of the PTA. The superintendent must always keep in mind that although many constituencies must be dealt with, two are primary. First and foremost, the chief school officer is the advocate for all of the children in the district. At the same time, it cannot be forgotten that a superintendent holds a responsibility to the elected board of education. On occasion it will be necessary to speak for the children even when some or all board members are thinking differently about an issue. These are times when the superintendent becomes the true leader of the district. The danger always exists that such a difference can cause the superintendent to lose the support of some of the board members. Still, if the chief school officer is truly an advocate for children, conflict will be inevitable. At such a time, the leader of the district must attempt to demonstrate courage as Ernest Hemingway defined it. John Kennedy used the author's definition of courage in his book *Profiles in Courage*. For Hemingway, courage was "grace under pressure." A superintendent must remain calm in the face of strong opposition in these times of conflict.

Of course, public confrontations are best avoided whenever possible. One way to help prevent conflict is to ensure that information is made available to everyone. Superintendents should be visible in the district as guest speakers for community groups. At these events it is extremely important to be well prepared and to use the occasion to talk about not only the good things being done by students and teachers but also the district's future plans and objectives.

Another method for reaching the community is by utilizing a district newsletter and also the local media. Both of these outlets can be used to highlight the positive activities taking place in the schools. Still, it is important that the information not always sound like a prepared commercial. The tone of press releases and newsletters should read as a neutral reporting of school news.

Gaining fair press coverage should be a goal of the superintendents. To that end, it is important not to treat reporters as the enemy. They are people with an important job to do, and a superintendent should help rather than hinder them in meeting their responsibilities. Treating reporters in a friendly, respectful, and helpful manner is a wiser course than trying to fool or intimidate them. Even though any district obviously wishes to avoid negative media coverage, the superintendent should not try to hide bad news or be defensive. Most important, it is essential that an administrator not bend the truth to avoid criticism. Losing one's reputation for credibility and integrity should not be traded for a temporary reprieve from unfavorable criticism. Frequent use of "no comment" responses can often make it appear that the district is attempting to hide a problem. On the other hand, when answering a question by a reporter, the superintendent should be concise and to the point. This approach is especially important when being interviewed for radio or television, as whatever answer is given should fit into a very short sound bite.

With the media, the superintendent should most often be the spokesperson for the board of education. When doing so, the chief school officer must defend board decisions even when he or she might have reservations about their wisdom. If a superintendent disagrees with the board of education, a private discussion should take place. Any superintendent who makes such differences public should be ready to look for a new position.

The superintendent also should not attempt to transfer the blame for a school district problem to someone else. As chief school officer, the responsibility for everything that happens will fall on the superintendent's shoulders. There will be times when it will be necessary to take the heat for others' mistakes.

Finally, do not try to duck too many questions posed by reporters. Whenever possible, a superintendent should prepare for the inevitable questions that reporters will ask. When something happens in a school, it is essential to learn the facts quickly and prepare for a call from a reporter. If it is impossible to obtain a complete account of the problem, avoid making comments that will later be proven incorrect.

As the educational leader in the district, the superintendent will address questions concerning many issues facing the community. Politically it is probably best to keep personal political affiliations and partisan views private. As superintendent, one has a responsibility to all people in the district and not just to a single political party. In dealing with municipal leaders, it is important to be respectful and open. All school employees should be encouraged to interact regularly with representatives of other municipal governments. Principals, guidance counselors, and psychologists should be working closely with social workers, probation officers, and representatives of the local child protection agency. Superintendents or designated members of the administrative team should attend local government meetings and hearings that might affect the school district.

Along with government officials, the chief school officer should pay attention to the business community. It helps to have the school district represented on the chamber of commerce and the junior chamber of commerce.

Local businesspeople can be allies to public education, but too often if barred from participation from school business, they can also become critics. Area businesses can provide student job programs, shadowing opportunities, and speakers at school career days and become members of school advisory committees. At times they donate to school causes, advertise in publications, or provide scholarships. Some businesses have given used equipment to schools. One sensitive problem related to local businesses is whether the school district purchases locally. Needless to say, when a local business is competitive, they should be given strong consideration when purchasing either goods or services.

Local business organizations and civic clubs are very likely to invite a new school superintendent to join their group. Most Kiwanis, Rotary, and Lions Clubs would be happy to claim a new school administrator as a member. A word of caution is necessary. Although it might seem politically wise to join one or more influential groups in the community, a superintendent must be careful with his or her schedule. Of special concern are the groups that meet weekly, either at lunch or in the evening. Such a commitment can be more than a busy administrator will be able to meet, given the schedule of school-related events. Certainly, if a superintendent does agree to join such an organization, he or she should make it clear that attending all meetings is likely to be impossible. Of course, missing meetings with some of these groups only means making them up in another community or paying fines. In addition to the regular meetings, the organizations are also active in doing service projects, which can cut into one's schedule. To join and be a less than fully involved member of a civic organization might be worse than not joining at all. Whatever the decision, it would be wise not to accept membership in any community group until one has time to understand school commitments. A new superintendent might expect that the contacts made in such an organization would help provide a political base of support for a superintendent within a community. Perhaps it can be helpful if a person stays long enough in a district, but when a superintendent does get into trouble, often the club members do not come forward to defend the beleaguered administrator. The decision to be part of a local civic club should only be made if an administrator enjoys this type of activity and can become an effective member.

A similar issue can occur when one considers joining a church, synagogue, or other religious institution. If membership in a religious group is something that is meaningful, it is essential to choose the affiliation that best meets an administrator's personal spiritual needs. If that can be done within the school district, it is probably prudent to worship regularly with members of the community. On the other hand, to choose a congregation based on political expediency is probably unwise. If a new superintendent needs to leave the district to find an appropriate place to worship, the board of education and the members of the community will most often accept this choice. Being uncomfortable in a congregation even though it is located in one's school district will make attendance less rewarding and in the long run be more of a chore than a comfort.

While any administrator should be cautious about joining community groups, a superintendent needs to be active in participating in school-related activities. As the chief school officer, one should develop a professional relationship with parent–teacher organizations. It is important to be visible at some of the meetings and attempt to participate in fund-raising activities. It is a good idea to attend meetings at different schools and not to forget a group even though it is small. Superintendents must also be open to discussions with booster groups, alumni organizations, and school district foundations.

When attending local functions, parents and citizens will attempt to share their concerns about school programs and personnel. Also, in some communities, people will call the superintendent at home to discuss their problems with schools. This is especially true in small districts where the chief school officer lives in the community. Although such calls indicate that people believe that their administration is approachable, they sometimes can be difficult. A superintendent must be careful about what is said during these informal conversations. If the person has not yet discussed the problem with the principal or the appropriate department manager, a referral to the individual with direct responsibility over the matter can be a proper response. If taking this approach, the superintendent should inform the supervisor of the matter immediately. During such a discussion it is important to ask for a report on how the matter is resolved. Sometimes the complaint cannot be delegated. When being told about a potential problem, most often it is helpful to ask for some time to investigate the matter. After involving the appropriate school personnel, an attempt should be made to resolve the matter as quickly as possible. It is important, then, to notify the individual making the complaint of the action that is being taken. It will undoubtedly be impossible to satisfy everyone who asks the superintendent for intervention, but they must know that an attempt has been made to deal with the issue.

One of the most difficult groups to deal with in any community is an organization that has as its primary purpose lowering taxes. Such a group can be critical not only of the school but of the superintendent personally.

Even though they can be easily seen as the enemy, it is important to be open with information and respectful to the members of the organization. If such a group is using the media to spread inaccurate information, it must be publicly refuted using the school district newsletter or special releases. Such rebuttals need only to correct inaccurate information, avoiding excessive rhetoric. A superintendent should be especially cautious in dealing with published letters to the editor. By responding to such a critical letter in the same newspaper, the administrator can be caught in an extended letter-writing exchange. Although such an ongoing debate could help sell some newspapers, it probably is not a particularly good forum for a superintendent.

It is important for a superintendent to be an active participant in the community dialogue concerning education. This can be done as a guest editorialist in a newspaper or as a speaker to community organizations. At the same time, a chief school officer can be visible to the public in numerous other ways. Whether it is as a participant at a senior faculty benefit basketball game, a guest conductor at a concert, or the person who welcomes groups using the school buildings, the chief school officer should be seen as the spokesperson and leader of the district. In doing so, one can either foster the interest of the children of the district or become a detriment to them. An individual cannot be a truly successful superintendent without being able to mobilize a community in a joint commitment to their children. As administrators we need to remember the African proverb that Hillary Clinton used as the title for her book, *It Takes a Whole Village to Raise the Child.* Superintendents must be leaders in bringing communities together to meet this important responsibility.

CHAPTER THIRTEEN

The Superintendent and Technology

Like the leaders in all organizations in our society, superintendents are being affected by changes in technology. In the past thirty years, the computer has impacted almost every phase of a school administrator's job. Beginning in the late 1960s, computers began to be used in an ever-increasing number of management functions. Perhaps the first application was in secondary school student scheduling. Soon after, computer programs were developed for record storage, payroll, accounting, budget development, and even bus routes. More recently, districts have set up their own Web sites to communicate with community members who have their own home computers. These sites make information available to residents about the district as well as schedules of activities.

For management functions, the computer gives administrators and board members a huge amount of information that can be used to make decisions. Also important is the fact that the information is easily and quickly accessible. It is no longer necessary for a superintendent to wait for the monthly budget report to know exactly how much money has been expended in a particular budget line. The many exhausting hours spent by guidance counselors and building principals dealing with scheduling conflicts has been greatly reduced. Because of the Internet, superintendents can receive instant information from other schools as well as their state education department. Fax machines, e-mail, and conference calls have also added to the possibilities for more rapid and less expensive communication.

Despite the advantages of the new technology, it also poses a number of potential problems. Callers are often frustrated and confused by the many options given on a recorded message. Many people would rather speak to a real person when they call the school.

A second possible problem is the case of managers who have become so involved with their computers that it has reduced their direct contact

with others. It has been reported that some school administrators are trying to manage via e-mail. High-paid administrators spend significant
amounts of time slowly and with little skill typing material that was once
prepared more quickly and accurately by professional secretaries. The result of such practices can be a more impersonal office environment.

There is also the potential of creating information overload. Some
budgeting programs give numerous report options that managers can find
overwhelming. Despite this and the other potential pitfalls to technology,
however, there is no question that a superintendent during the twenty-first
century will have to be computer-literate.

At some point in a chief school officer's preparation, it is necessary to
develop skills and learn the vocabulary of technology. This expertise will
be true for performing not only the management functions in schools but
also the role of instructional leader.

During the 1990s, billions of dollars were spent to ensure that every
school building in the United States had computers. The support for this
initiative has come from government at the federal, state, and local levels.
Computerization has also been extremely popular with local taxpayers.
Districts that have had trouble gaining support for their annual budget
have been able to gain approval of large bond issues to finance technology. Community members are well aware from their own personal experience that the computer has become an essential tool in our society. Parents want their children to be competitive in this technological
environment. There are many additional reasons for the fact that computers are a popular motivation in our schools.

To begin with, nearly all young people like to use them. Students are
more likely to do writing assignments if they can be done on a computer.
The interactive potential of a computer allows for the development of drill
and practice exercises that are often more popular with students than
doing paper-and-pencil assignments. In addition, classroom computers
give teachers another tool for individualizing instruction within our increasingly diverse classrooms. Specially designed software programs can
be extremely effective for teaching children with learning disabilities or
for challenging gifted and talented students. Perhaps most important is the
potential of technology to allow children to engage in creative problem
solving.

Advocates of computer-assisted technology insist that it can free teachers from being primarily "information givers" and allow them to become
facilitators of learning. With the Internet, every student has an ever-
increasing amount of information available. Children can utilize the best

sources from all over the world and communicate with others in far away places. All of this potential causes many to believe that computers will help make our children excited about a lifetime of learning. More than just preparing them for future jobs, we can create the interest and develop the skills that will make their lives richer and the world a better place.

Another potential blessing of technology was introduced during the past twenty-five years. Distance learning is an innovation that has moved from simple television videotapes to sophisticated interactive classes between teachers and students. Schools and colleges are now providing entire courses over the Web. From the syllabus to the final examination, students and teachers are communicating solely through the Internet. In the April 2000 edition of *The Journal,* Sylvia Charp describes the characteristics that make distance learning programs successful:

1. Clearly defined performance- and competency-based objectives that are understood by both instructor and learner
2. Acceptance of students with the background, knowledge, and technical skills needed to undertake the program
3. Manageable class size—fifteen to thirty students
4. Instructors available at regular, stated hours
5. Institution evaluates its programs' educational effectiveness, including assessment of student learning objectives[1]

In this article, Charp shares the Merrill Lynch prediction that spending on technology-delivered education will grow from $3.0 billion in 1998 to $8.2 billion in 2001.[2]

Perhaps one of the newest ways to use computers for instruction is in the area of faculty development. Increasingly, teachers are learning online. In the Allen Independent School District outside Dallas, one of their goals for 2000 was to "help teachers by putting all their staff development on-line. With Lotus Learning Space, teachers will be able to assess all their professional development on-line at their convenience instead of having to sit in classrooms or stay after school."[3] The district will also use Learning Space to put their own courses on the Web. In the future, the computer will likely be used increasingly as a tool for staff development, especially for courses that help integrate technology into individual classrooms.

Still another form of technology for improving teaching is the use of videotape. In an article published in the May 2000 issue of *Educational Leadership,* Miriam Gamoran Sherin talks about video clubs that help "teachers gain opportunities to investigate their teaching practices and to better understand what is happening in their classroom."[4]

Even with its great potential for education, serious concerns are being voiced about the use of technology as a primary educational tool. Superintendents must be aware of what these critics are saying.

Currently, although most middle- and upper-class families have one or more computers in their home, millions of other children still do not have easy access to computers outside school. Like other implications of our seemingly growing gap between the haves and the have nots, lack of computer availability does put many children at a decided disadvantage. At least one school has sought to remedy this problem. The Carmen Arace Middle School in Bloomfield, Connecticut, has made available a laptop computer to virtually every one of its nearly nine hundred students. In addition, laptops are available in classrooms, in the library, and even on school buses. The school, which contains ninety percent minority students, has provided the following to its students:

1. a rugged notebook computer for every student and teacher; the computers are "child proof," which is almost a necessity in a middle school setting
2. an infrared wireless connection to the school's local area network; no need to plug in the computers—and no danger of tripping over wires— at school or in the home
3. a low-cost, high-speed Internet connection; students have access to the almost unlimited resources of the World Wide Web
4. ongoing support and professional development[5]

This middle school has taken the time to develop a comprehensive technology plan. Too many school districts have moved into technology without developing a vision or a long-range strategy. In preparing such a plan, districts should take advantage of the technological knowledge of community members as well as the faculty and staff. These groups should be given a clear-cut mission by the superintendent along with any support that is needed.

First and foremost, an advisory committee must chart some long-range objectives for the use of technology in the district. The plan should pay special attention to the need for an ongoing program of faculty and staff training. Without a major commitment to educating teachers and staff, any plan is likely to be doomed. The staff development component of a technology plan must be carefully crafted to encourage employees. Mandatory classes at the end of a workday are not the best answer. Paid workshops, perhaps during the summer, are better alternatives. Special financial grants to faculty members who are able to devise creative ways to use technology in the classroom can also provide motivation for experimentation. Forcing all teachers to move at the same pace will undoubtedly meet with resistance. Administrators must be aware of the need for sensitivity and positive reinforcement as teachers gradually introduce new technology into their classroom.

Any technology plan will also need to address a program for expanding the inventory of hardware and software and for the need to frequently update obsolete equipment. Of course, along with the necessity to update equipment, the skills of the faculty and staff will also need to be increased. It is not enough to have training when new programs are introduced. Technological staff development must be ongoing.

Along with the need for a plan and constant in-service training, districts must also be on guard for the misuse of computers. Computers in libraries and labs are frequently not well supervised; as a result, students are using them to play games or aimlessly surf the 'Net. More dangerous is the possibility that they are visiting sites that are inappropriate. Such problems lead to the issue of blocking. Superintendents and other administrators are faced with the dilemma of balancing their responsibility to create a wholesome learning environment with the desire not to become a censor. In his article "Beyond the Blocking Solution," Paul Lynch suggests that "the debate over student access to the Internet should be discussed in the language and discipline of our trade—as a curricular and instructional challenge."[6] Lynch argues that "managed Internet use starts with the exact opposite position from blocking software. It starts with an empty arena to which teachers add curriculum-related sites. With this method, when a teacher wants students to analyze and compare three Internet sources, only these three sources are available to students."[7]

This solution would limit a student's use of the Internet to specific age-appropriate, curriculum-based sites. Many administrators would find such limitations too restrictive. On the other hand, we cannot have our sixth graders sitting at a computer in the school library viewing pornography.

Administrators are also concerned that currently sufficient software is not available to help students meet the academic standards set by their states. Without appropriate and effective software to help meet these new standards, classroom computers will become less important. Because individual states each have their own standards, such software will be most effective if it is customized for individual states. This matter will be a major challenge for state education departments. If teachers are going to be evaluated based on their students' success in "high-stakes" examinations, they are going to need materials that target these curriculum goals.

Increasingly, articles in major educational journals are questioning our national fascination with technology in the schools. One such article appeared in the February 1999 issue of *Educational Digest.* The author makes a strong case for the continued use of paper textbooks. Ruth Wisengrad cites another article entitled "The Computer Delusion," which appeared as a cover story in the *Atlantic Monthly* in July 1997. In this story, Ted Oppenheimer points out that in the 1920s, Thomas Edison and others predicted that movies and radio would soon replace the textbook. In the 1960s, psychologist B. F. Skinner wrote that teaching machines and programmed learning would greatly enhance our educational program. Of course, educational television was also supposed to revolutionize the classroom. In the *Atlantic Monthly* article, Jamie McKenzie contends that even with all of the new technological teaching tools, including the computer, the traditional textbook remains an extremely important way for students to learn. They "provide information that has been expertly researched and consolidated for various levels of understanding . . . and they filter, they focus, they organize and they deliver complex subjects like U.S. History and Biology in manageable, digestible chunks and bites."[8] Wisengrad concludes her article by quoting William L. Ruckeyser, who said, "a basic truth in education is that a child must be literate before he or she is computer literate. And the best teacher has always been a person, not a machine."[9]

In another article, Susan Nelson attacks the validity of the technological initiative in our schools. She claims that "many young people today are doing little important work" on computers "that could not be done otherwise. Chatrooms, games, and Internet advertisement masquerading as something else are hardly what anyone envisioned or intended for kids."[10] As one of a number of critics of the increasing use of technology in schools, the author states that her "primary concern with the advancement of the Internet in schools is the impact it will have on the way students in the new millennium will think. If we teach students to be merely information gatherers without teaching them to think critically and to evaluate the information they get, we are doing them a disservice."[11]

Superintendents in the years ahead will have to think carefully about what computers and other technology can and cannot accomplish in the classroom. Hard choices will have to be made. It appears now that limiting class size in the primary grades can lead to increased academic growth for children. Would we be better off spending our limited funds on new teachers rather than on machines that will soon be outdated? Would investment in ongoing staff development for our faculty also be a more effective way to increase student achievement? These are questions educational leaders must ask as they consider putting more dollars into technology.

Even though it is important to critically consider and compare educational initiatives, technology will remain a priority program in our schools for the foreseeable future. Tom Payzant, in an article entitled "Superintendents: Empowering with Technology," reminds us that we must always remember that "the goal is to improve teaching and learning."[12] Computers are just one tool to be used in meeting this, our primary objective.

It will be the superintendent's role to attempt to ensure that a proper balance is maintained between the use of the new technology and what has traditionally served us well in our classrooms. From the challenge of technology, we now turn to more personal issues facing those who wish to be superintendents in the twenty-first century.

NOTES

1. Sylvia Charp, "Distance Education," *The Journal* (April 2000): 10.

2. Charp, "Distance Education," 10.

3. Penny Jones, "The Power of Web Collaboration," *The Journal* (May 2000): 34–35.

4. Miriam Gamoran Sherin, "Viewing Teaching in Videotape," *Educational Leadership* (May 2000): 36.

5. Ian Elliot, "A Laptop in Every Backpack," *Teaching K–8* (April 2000): 42.

6. Paul Lynch, "Beyond the Blocking Solution," *The Journal* (March 2000): 80.

7. Lynch, "Beyond the Blocking Solution," 82.

8. Ruth Wisengrad, "Are Textbooks Ready to Fold?" *Educational Digest* (February 1999): 59.

9. Wisengrad, "Are Textbooks Ready to Fold?" 61.

10. Susan Nelson, "Technology in Schools: Whose Best Interest?" *Educational Digest* (May 2000): 46.

11. Nelson: 47.

12. Justine K. Brown, "Superintendents: Empowering with Technology," *Converge*, May 2000: 52.

CHAPTER FOURTEEN

The Superintendent's Personal Life

One of the greatest challenges for superintendents is to balance the demands of their many professional responsibilities with the need to live a full and rich life away from the office. Perhaps the first major issue that must be faced is to decide where to live. In the past, it was not unusual for the district to provide a home for its superintendent, often located near one of the schools. This practice of providing housing for superintendents is becoming a thing of the past, but many school systems still require the superintendent to reside in the district. Even if it is not a mandate outlined in the contract, many board members continue to feel strongly that their superintendent should live in the community.

Increasingly, some superintendents are seeking to establish their residence outside the school district in which they work. These individuals may feel a need to ensure additional privacy in their lives. If they have a family, they sometimes argue that their children would face unwanted scrutiny and pressure because their parent was the superintendent. They may also fear that their children's behavior will be judged by a higher standard than that of their peers. In addition, it can be awkward for the superintendent who is a parent of students within the district. For instance, it could be difficult during a parent conference for teachers when the parent is the superintendent. Finally, some would contend that living outside the school district allows an administrator to have a more normal lifestyle. It is possible to go to the store without worrying about changing clothes. People would not necessarily be gauging one's weekly church attendance. Living outside the district would certainly eliminate the possible charges of favoritism that can occur if an administrator's children attend the district schools. It is also likely that a superintendent living outside the district will not be interrupted by as many calls during the dinner hour. All of these factors and more can present personal problems for a superintendent.

On the other hand, there are many reasons for considering residence in the school district. Perhaps one of the most compelling is the fact that many board members and people in the community appreciate having their superintendent close by. Other residents believe that an administrator will care more about the school if he or she is a parent whose own children attend. Especially in smaller districts, the superintendent might be the highest-paid public servant, some people believe that a person in this role has a responsibility to be active in the community. In addition, very likely past superintendents have lived in the district.

Professionally, interacting on a daily basis with district residents has its advantages. By being visible and active, an administrator has a better chance of knowing the concerns of the community. When one becomes a fixture in a neighborhood, in local stores and restaurants, as well as in church and civic organizations, people will feel more comfortable sharing their concerns. The level of trust that people feel toward a superintendent will grow if they view their chief school officer as an active and caring person and not merely another official sitting behind a desk. Knowing what people are thinking can only help any administrator make better decisions and develop more effective strategies for change.

Here again, a word of caution is needed. Perhaps an administrator's most persistent source of information will come from discussions at the family dinner table. These communications must be dealt with in a very sensitive manner. It is essential that confidential information not be discussed with one's children. It is important that they not be led to believe that their complaints will automatically cause their parent to fire a teacher or principal. Family members' comments need to be treated the same way as those of other members of the community. The fact remains that administrators will probably be surprised some days by what is said at their dinner table.

Finally, and perhaps most important, it can be argued that living in the district can enrich one's life and help develop a strong sense of community. Because of the common interests shared by the family, there is not a separation between the administrator's professional and personal life. Whether or not one lives in the district, any move to a new community can cause problems. Today one of the most common complications that occurs is when a spouse has a career in the community from which the administrator is moving. Frequently it is extremely difficult to find a comparable position in the new district. As a result, more often than in the past many couples are living apart for significant lengths of time. Sometimes it is only months, but for others it becomes a way of life. The children are also affected when an administrator takes a new job, which can especially be a problem for adolescent children. One must be careful to weigh these factors when the family is considering a move.

A relatively new phenomenon has been the decision of some superintendents to take a new job in a higher-paying district during the final few years of their career. Many of these individuals do so to boost their final average salary for retirement purposes. In New York state, it is not unusual for even small districts on Long Island to pay salaries $30,000 to $40,000 higher than similar-sized upstate districts. Consequently, a number of individuals at age fifty-two have taken a position on Long Island and have commuted to upstate New York on weekends. One should think long and hard about such a decision.

All of the issues surrounding the choice of residence for superintendents can be crucial in affecting an administrator's happiness and effectiveness. If a superintendent is considering staying in a district for a time and possibly planning this job as the final position during his or her career, the argument for living in the community is even stronger. Not every superintendent needs to live in the district in which he or she works. This decision must be carefully considered. Many superintendents feel that being part of the community is not only helpful but a positive experience for the whole family.

Another concern directly related to the choice of residence is the personal relationships that are developed. The community will observe closely the people with whom superintendents spend their time, especially if these people are members of the board of education, the faculty, or the staff. With such relationships, it is important to be concerned about the appearance of favoritism toward these individuals. Of course, superintendents in neighboring districts are certainly people who will have common interests. If possible, fostering friendships with people outside the field of education is healthy.

Because of the nature of the superintendency, one will have hundreds of acquaintances. However, for many of us this is not enough. For most administrators, it is also important to develop and cultivate some lasting friendships. Although superintendents are often social people, their busy schedules and the need to be discreet about their work make it difficult to develop close friendships. Too often, superintendents work in a community for many years and still fail to establish roots. The fact that many career-oriented administrators frequently move from district to district makes it even more difficult for them to have real friends. The failure to take the time for friendship becomes painfully evident when superintendents retire and feel that they are more alone in their own community than they ever anticipated.

Although friendships are important, an administrator must always remain close to his or her family. For those administrators who are married, the role of the superintendent's partner is changing. In the past, it was quite common for the board of education to meet a candidate's partner as part of the interviewing process, informally or at a more formal dinner with board members. Even though today many superintendents' spouses have their own careers, certain community expectations still persist. Although entertaining board members and school personnel is not required, some superintendents still do so on occasion. At formal events such as retirement parties, superintendents' partners are usually in attendance. Before one seeks to become a chief school officer, the entire family needs to understand that certain unique expectations and demands will be placed on them.

As a superintendent develops a weekly schedule, it certainly should include evenings at home. If one has a family, they should be the top priority. Children grow up very quickly, and administrators can live to regret not spending enough time with them.

On those quiet nights at home, there will also be educational books and journals to be read. This is a professional responsibility that cannot be neglected, but it should not occur by compromising time with one's family.

However important it is to remain informed in the field of education, it is equally essential that a superintendent have other interests. Whether it is reading history, painting, playing the piano, flying an airplane, or working in the garden, an administrator needs to spend recreational time away from the job. As a professional, a school leader will also be expected to be knowledgeable about current events. Few people are as boring as an individual who can talk about only one subject.

Another important concern will affect an administrator's ability to do the job. Medical authorities are unanimous in the need to schedule time for regular exercise. It is not enough to engage in a sport every other week. Whether it be before school or after school, it is helpful to set aside a block of time at least five days a week to ensure that an individual remains physically fit. We can all find excuses for not exercising, but it is a major mistake not to make the time. If the activity can be done with a partner or a friend, it might be easier, but often a solitary workout can be an excellent time for quiet reflection. With so many demands on a superintendent's time, it is essential that a schedule be devised that takes into account the need for exercise and time with family and friends.

Especially during the first year on the job, the demands on a new superintendent will be overwhelming. There will be numerous invitations to speak to both school organizations and community groups. Most of these invitations should be accepted. Needless to say, a new chief school officer will also want to attend a number of school athletic events, concerts, plays, and PTA meetings. It is likely that a superintendent's schedule might include attending multiple events on the same evening.

Possibly during the first year a new administrator will be unable to plan a reasonable schedule. After that time, superintendents should make some critical decisions as to how they will spend their evenings. In doing so, commitments with the board of education need to be at the top of the list. Almost everything else is optional. It is important to be visible at school events, but there is a need to be selective. If a parent, the first priority should be to attend events in which your children are participating. Many superintendents regret that as parents, they did not take more time to attend the activities of their children. Although some children will never specifically ask their parents to come to a game or another school event, most would really like them to be there.

While choosing events, it is important to remember that even though one may love basketball, the wrestling and swimming teams also appreciate seeing an administrator at their events. Of course, it is necessary to attend both boys' and girls' events. As one settles into a position, it will become clear that it is unnecessary and perhaps impossible to attend every Friday evening football or basketball game, unless these events are truly a favored recreation for an administrator's family.

Only after commitments with the board of education, family, and friends are actually put on the calendar should other school- and community-related events be scheduled. This advice is almost impossible to take, but unless an administrator continually makes his or her personal life a priority, professional obligations can totally dominate a superintendent's time.

The job of a superintendent is so demanding that many chief school officers fail to take the vacation days they are allotted. Board of education members will not begrudge administrators who take time off. It will not appear in one's obituary that he or she had not taken 104 of the allotted vacation days. The fact is that vacations are necessary to anyone's physical and mental health. The time off provides administrators the opportunity for relaxation, reflection, and additional experiences with family and friends. Although some superintendents take their vacation a day or two at a time, such a practice often does not really allow one to get away from the job. Frequently, leaving the community provides the only true escape for a school administrator.

In conclusion, a superintendent must learn to use personal time in a wise manner. Too many administrators allow the job to become the primary focus of their lives. As a result, they are more likely to burn out, have family problems, and become driven and boring people. One cannot emphasize too much the need for a well-rounded lifestyle that allows the superintendent to become a complete human being.

CHAPTER FIFTEEN

Career Choices

During a person's career as a superintendent, an individual will consider the possibility of seeking a position in another district. This is especially true if the superintendent is relatively young when accepting their first position as a chief school officer. Someone in their thirties or forties is bound to wonder, "Do I want to do this the rest of my life?" As a superintendent attempts to answer this question, weighing the pros and cons of making a change becomes necessary.

Staying in a district for an extended period of time or even for an entire career holds many advantages. Chief among these is the stability it provides for an administrator and for a family. Moving from community to community is especially traumatic if a superintendent has children. Especially if an administrator has teenagers, their friends and activities often tie them to a community. Today there is also a serious problem of uprooting one's spouse from a career. Selling a home at a fair price can also be a tedious task. Frequent moves make it more difficult to develop and maintain friendships. Professionally a superintendent may have begun projects in a district that he or she would like to see completed. Finally, the routine developed in a district may be more comfortable and less stressful than taking on a new position.

There is also a real advantage to putting down roots in a community. This point is especially true if one is working in a location close to extended family members. A time will come when it is helpful to be near parents as they age. Frequent gatherings of relatives create traditions that tie families together. Superintendents living in communities far from their families often lose the closeness and comfort of special times with their relatives.

In addition, staying in one community can allow a superintendent to nurture lifelong friendships. One cannot overemphasize this advantage. The school administrator who moves from district to district can have a difficult time creating and maintaining lasting friendships. It can be done, but one must make a real effort to keep in touch with those in former communities where the superintendent might have lived.

Finally, there is the pleasure and comfort of familiarity. Going to the same doctor and dentist for decades or to a favorite restaurant on special occasions is important to some people. As one becomes tied to the community, it is easier to identify with local athletic teams and to enjoy the annual schedule of community events. The homecoming football game, the Memorial Day parade, and class reunions become a regular part of one's life. Especially after a number of years in a district, it is rewarding to talk with graduates who return to the school and community. All of these things can be sources of satisfaction for a school superintendent who remains in one community.

On the other hand, staying in a district for an extended period of time can have a number of disadvantages. After the "honeymoon," the option of escape sometimes seems an attractive alternative in the face of persistent critics and difficult faculty and staff members. It is all but impossible to be in a leadership role in a school district without experiencing situations that will create detractors and critics. Decisions cannot be made without upsetting someone. For a superintendent remaining for an extended time in a district, the list of unhappy constituents is bound to grow.

Sometimes superintendents, like anyone else who stays in a job for a long period, will feel that they are in a rut. The repetitive pattern of the school calendar can cause such feelings. After one has been through hundreds of board of education and PTA meetings, these activities can become less than stimulating. After having given numerous speeches on opening day and graduation, it is often difficult to think of something new to say. When one has been the guest speaker at the local Kiwanis Club for the sixth time, a superintendent might well wish for a different audience.

Of course, there will be people in the school organization from whom a chief school officer might also like to escape—perhaps an overly assertive union representative or a superintendent of buildings and grounds who is always complaining about the students. Maybe a local newspaper editor or reporter loves to criticize the superintendent and the board of education.

Running away from unpleasant people is not the best reason for seeking a new position. For many, the primary reason for moving is ambition. One probably would not have reached a position as a chief school officer without being strongly motivated by the prospect of leadership. In public schools, a superintendent's status is most often gauged by the size of the school district. It is also true that frequently, larger districts pay higher salaries. It is not unusual for an administrator in a district with 1,000 students to be looking for an opportunity in a community with 2,500 children. The best-paying jobs tend to be in affluent suburban areas. In our society where professional recognition is based on salary and the size of the organization being managed, it is not surprising that ambitious superintendents seek to move to larger districts.

A decision to move to another community should be made carefully. One must think about the frequency of the career changes being made. Although school administration is a career in which mobility is expected, one can move too often. School boards are likely to look askance at a candidate who has a track record that includes changes every two or three years. An inspiring administrator would hopefully stay in a position long enough to be able to point to a number of significant accomplishments.

In the field of educational administration, one's background is also an important factor. If an individual has been appointed to a superintendency without a doctorate, the first decision that will need to be made is whether to return for additional graduate work. Should professional or personal aspirations cause an individual to again become a student, one's life and priorities will be greatly affected. Before such a decision is made, it should be discussed with family members and with the board of education. Unless a superintendency is being sought in a large district or an individual wishes to someday enter college teaching, the doctorate is not a prerequisite for achieving positions that offer outstanding compensation and challenges. Some moderately large districts will hire someone without a doctorate. The level of cost and commitment in both money and time will be substantial, and thus a decision to seek an advanced degree is a serious one for any school administrator.

In deciding on an advanced degree or a change of districts, the question to ask is whether the individual and family will be happier as a result of the change. Moving just to increase one's income by $20,000 a year or to build up a final average salary for retirement is probably not enough to justify uprooting a family. The apparent added prestige of being a chief school officer in a larger district may not be worth the additional stress created by the new position.

Perhaps the best reason for considering a move is if the superintendent is a person who is seeking new challenges and feels that he or she can make a positive difference in a new district. If this is the case, a person will obviously wish to leave the current community when things are going well rather than during a crisis. Those individuals hoping to make a change need to keep in mind several factors.

The first and most important requirement is to do well in the current job and to be able to show some specific accomplishments to prospective employers. Districts are seeking leaders who have had measurable impact on their previous school systems. Without a record of successes, even the most persuasive candidate will be less than convincing.

It is also necessary to have a number of individuals who will act as references. This group can include board members, university professors, community leaders, or possibly administrators, faculty, or staff members from previous districts in which a candidate has worked. Any job candidate should ask potential references in advance whether they are willing to be a positive reference. Choosing the best references is important. They need to be people who are truly enthusiastic about the candidate's leadership. In addition, they should be respected individuals who can articulate clearly what the candidate has to offer to a school district. What they write or say personally will be critical to any person seeking an administrative position.

To obtain a better job, it is helpful to develop a network of colleagues. This can be done by becoming active in regional and state administrative and school board organizations. Such activities can also help superintendents to remain well informed about educational trends outside the district. There is, however, the danger that too much of this kind of activity can be seen in a district as detracting from one's job. This is especially true if these responsibilities force an individual to travel outside the district frequently. A superintendent cannot afford to be seen as an absentee leader.

If so inclined, a superintendent can also help build a strong résumé by writing articles for educational journals or making presentations at professional meetings. Both activities can enhance one's reputation and give positive publicity to a district. For the ambitious school administrator, it is extremely helpful to have his or her district seen as being exceptional. Both within the superintendent's own community and with professional colleagues, articles and presentations will also help someone seeking a new position be regarded as an innovator and a leader.

When considering a move, the chief school officer should be cautious about sharing this desire. One's candidacy for a new position, especially in a nearby district, is difficult to keep secret. It is essential to have a plan as to who will be informed of your application and at what point in the process they are to be told. It can be harmful to a superintendent for board of education members to learn through the "rumor mill" that their chief school officer is seeking another position. It is best to say that another school district has shown an interest and that you are merely exploring the possibilities. Unfortunately, other districts do not often make the first move to recruit a superintendent. Most superintendents have to seek out new positions, but if a friend or acquaintance does recommend an administrator's name to another district, it is possible that an invitation to apply will be extended.

Superintendents seeking to move should be selective, both in the specific district they are considering and in the timing of their move. One should learn as much as possible about a district before becoming a candidate. There are several important areas to explore:

1. Why is the incumbent superintendent leaving?
2. What has been the history of the superintendent in the district? What has been the rate of turnover?
3. What is the history and current status of labor relations in the district?
4. What is the level of academic achievement in the district?
5. To what degree has the community been supportive of the district budget and bond issues?
6. What is the present economic condition of the community?
7. What information is available about the current board of education in the district?

Answers to these questions can be found in state publications and in discussions with friends or professional colleagues who live in or near the district. It is not a bad idea to visit and get a feel of the community. This type of prior investigation might help a job candidate eliminate certain districts during a search for a new position.

When a superintendent becomes a serious candidate for another job, it is important to share this information with the board of education, as well as with key administrative team members. Because it is important not to be seen as dissatisfied with a current position, one seeking a new job should give a reasonable rationale for applying to another school district. Another reason for being selective and careful in becoming a candidate in other districts is that it can be harmful to be seen by others as a perennial job seeker. All superintendents should aspire to leave his or her present position without alienating those with whom one has worked. If an administrator is perceived as always being discontent or using threats of leaving to gain extra compensation, it is likely to create negative feelings within the district. Superintendents should do everything possible to leave a positive feeling about tenure in any district.

Although currently not as commonly as in the past, some superintendents decide to stay in one community for their entire career. Having made such a decision, there are several important issues to consider.

To avoid becoming stale and possibly bored, it is helpful to find some new challenges in one's professional and personal life. These can include new initiatives within the school system, as well as changes in the administrator's personal life. Some superintendents find it intellectually challenging to become mentors or supervisors for college graduate students who are doing internships. Teaching a class in one's own district or as an adjunct in a local college can add new life to a superintendent's schedule. This activity can also lead to improving the prospect of gaining a teaching position after retiring as a superintendent.

Taking a leadership role in the community, a professional organization, or a church can add a challenge to a superintendent seeking more than the regular routine of the job. These outside interests can lead to possible activities after retirement. Too many superintendents are bored after ending their careers because they have not thought about how they will spend their time after retirement. Although reading books and playing golf may seem like enough, retired superintendents sometimes suffer a letdown after leaving their positions. Following a career that mandated a busy schedule, some are unhappy with a life that does not include frequent contact with others.

A retired superintendent can possibly become an interim administrator. Such assignments can be challenging and less stressful than a regular position. An interim superintendent can always leave an assignment if it becomes unbearable. Unfortunately, such work often entails more travel and even living away from home during the week. One needs to gauge the impact such an assignment will have on an administrator's personal life. Consulting work is also a possibility, but that, too, most often requires travel. Taking part-time jobs in fields unrelated to education or doing volunteer work are also popular choices for retiring superintendents. The most important consideration should be to have a plan for retirement. For those who fail to prepare, it is possible that the expected bliss and freedom will not occur and, rather, feelings of boredom and possibly depression will result.

This preparation also includes the need for financial planning. It is never too soon to consult a financial adviser to ensure an adequate source of supplementary retirement income. However generous a retirement plan might seem to be, it does not always adequately protect one against inflation. Do not wait until you are age fifty to begin saving for retirement.

These comments might lead a school administrator to conclude that it is possible to have a permanent plan for the future. The truth, of course, is that our lives and careers are not predictable and we do not totally control our own destiny. A career as a superintendent of schools is less secure than most. Problems in the school, a change in the board of education, or events in one's personal life can create the need to quickly change plans. As Lincoln lamented in a letter to Albert Hodges in 1864, "I claim not to have controlled events, but confess plainly that events have controlled me."[1] Whether it be because of a person's own inability to control events, personal errors, or mistakes by subordinates, it may be advisable and necessary for a superintendent to leave a district. For one's own personal mental health and that of the individual's family, a school administrator must accept such a situation and make the best of it. Frequently, this type of dilemma can lead to a change for the better.

Career plans and aspirations need to be constantly reevaluated. Still, an administrator cannot allow personal ambitions to affect daily decisions. Building a résumé must always be less important than building an outstanding school district. To do this, one must be an effective leader. This all-important fact is the subject of the next chapter.

NOTES

1. Editors of *Country Beautiful, Lincoln: His Words and His World* (Waukesha: Country Beautiful Foundations, 1965), 59.

CHAPTER SIXTEEN

Some Final Thoughts on Leadership

Often, a person beginning a career as a superintendent is enthusiastic and idealistic about the future. Most new superintendents are committed to making a positive difference in children's lives. For some, over a period of time the initial lofty goals are forgotten in an effort to merely survive in the position. The forces affecting a superintendent can become so strong that noble objectives are replaced by short-term tactics to ensure enough support just to keep the job. Like the politician who thinks primarily of the next election, a superintendent can focus on doing what is necessary to make certain that his or her contract is renewed. This can mean giving in or compromising on issues that could have a negative impact on children. Of course, compromise is necessary in any democracy, but a superintendent who cares primarily about his or her personal career is not really the type of leader that is needed in a school district.

What does leadership entail, and how can it make a difference? One of the ways to answer these questions is to look at the lives and careers of effective leaders. In the United States, most historians would agree that Abraham Lincoln would be such a leader. His career is replete with failures, but at each juncture in his life, he learned and grew. When he was elected president in 1860, his only experience at the national level was two years spent in the House of Representatives. Still, he was able to lead the country through perhaps the most critical period in our history. Generations of historians have attempted to articulate the reasons for Lincoln's greatness.

Many writers have argued that one of the reasons for his success was that he had clear objectives. If he could not heal the breach with the South that he inherited as president, Lincoln was totally committed to doing what was necessary to maintain the Union. Despite many early military defeats and increasing public criticism, he kept his focus on the vision of reuniting the nation. Later in the war, his goals were expanded to ending the institution of slavery, which he hated. With these dual purposes clearly in the forefront of his mind, he was able to steer the nation through the perilous years of the Civil War.

Having a clear vision would not have been enough if Lincoln had lacked political skills. He was an experienced politician who had an excellent sense of timing. Choosing to wait to issue the Emancipation Proclamation until the Union army had military success gave the policy greater credibility. He also was superb at choosing and managing his advisers. With a cabinet made up in large part of men who had been his rivals for the presidency, he was able to get his politically ambitious advisers to work hard and as a unit. In doing so, he eventually gained the respect and affection of these very talented men. As a leader, Lincoln was not afraid to make difficult personnel decisions. He replaced numerous generals of the Army of the Potomac before he found Ulysses S. Grant. Those he fired included George B. McClellan, who in 1864 nearly defeated Lincoln in his attempt to be reelected.

Lincoln's political skills included the ability to communicate in an eloquent but very clear manner. The ability to articulate the purposes of the war is evident not only in the Gettysburg Address but also in numerous other speeches and written documents. The Second Inaugural Address, with its call for a peaceful and forgiving reunion, was an effective attempt to set the tone for the difficult period that would follow the war. His many personal letters to friends and fellow citizens include numerous examples of his ability to communicate. Who could not be moved by this letter written to a mother whose sons had been lost in combat?

Dear Mrs. Bixby,

I have been shown in the files of the War Department a statement of the Adjutant General of Massachusetts, that you are the mother of five sons who have died gloriously on the field of battle.

I feel how weak and fruitless must be any words of mine which should attempt to beguile you from the grief of a loss so overwhelming. But I cannot refrain from tendering to you the consolation that may be found in the thanks of the Republic they died to save.

I pray that our Heavenly Father may assuage the anguish of your bereavement, and leave you only the cherished memory of the loved and lost, and the solemn pride that must be yours, to have laid so costly a sacrifice upon the altar of Freedom.

Yours, very sincerely and respectfully,
A. Lincoln[1]

The ability to touch people's hearts is something that will make someone a special leader.

Communication and political skills and a clear vision are still not enough to ensure that someone will be a successful leader. Adolf Hitler certainly had a vision for Germany. It was an evil plan, but he was certainly guided by it. He also had exceptional political skills, which allowed him to propel himself to absolute power in a chaotic political environment. What Hitler lacked was something that Lincoln had in abundance. From youth through his presidency, Lincoln had a reputation for honesty and integrity. Examples abound in Lincoln's career, as both a lawyer and a politician. Written when he was an attorney in Illinois, this letter represents the honesty for which Lincoln was famous.

Dear Sir:

I have just received your of 16th, with check on Flagg and Savage for twenty-five dollars. You must think I am a high-priced man. You are too liberal with your money. Fifteen dollars is enough for the job. I send you a receipt for fifteen dollars, and return to you a ten-dollar bill.

A. Lincoln[2]

Although some historians claim that Lincoln had many of the faults of other politicians, his life and leadership have stood the test of time and his reputation is still very much intact. He was a strong man who did not hesitate to use the powers of his office, but at the same time he remained a humble man who suffered with others. The troops in the field maintained their affection and respect for their commander in chief in large part because he was perceived as good and honest. Many other presidents have failed to inspire this type of support.

Several other characteristics can greatly aid any leader. Again turning to Lincoln, it is obvious that he did not take himself all that seriously. This quotation will suffice to demonstrate his self-effacing humility:

Dear Sir,

Your note requesting my "signature with a sentiment" was received, and should have been answered long since, but that it was mislaid. I am not a very sentimental man; and the best sentiment I can think of is, that if you collect the signatures of all persons who are no less distinguished than I, you will have a very undistinguishing mass of names.

A. Lincoln[3]

Lincoln also wrote about his own relationship with members of the female gender:

> Others have been made fools of by the girls, but this can never with truth be said of me. I most emphatically, in this instance, made a fool of myself. I have now come to the conclusion never again to think of marrying, and for this reason—I can never be satisfied with anyone who would be block-headed enough to have me.[4]

Lincoln's sense of humor is legendary. He frequently interrupted serious conversations to tell stories. Historian David Donald writes:

> Again and again self-important delegations would descend upon the White House, deliver themselves of ponderous utterances upon pressing issues of the war, and demand point-blank what the President proposed to do about their problems. Lincoln could say much in a few words when he chose, but he could also say nothing at great length when it was expedient. His petitioners' request, he would say, reminded him of "a little story," which he would proceed to tell in great detail, accompanied by mimicry and gestures, by hearty slapping of the thigh, by uproarious laughter at the end—at which time he would usher out his callers, baffled and confused by the smoke-screen of good humor, with their questions still unanswered.[5]

Humor was extremely important to Lincoln, as noted in this comment: "My father taught me how to work, but not to love it. I never did like to work, and I don't deny it. I'd rather read, tell stories, crack jokes, talk, laugh—anything but work."[6]

A sense of humor, humility, integrity, political skills, and vision were all characteristics that helped make Lincoln a great leader. Anyone aspiring to leadership can learn from the study of his life and the lives of other successful individuals. Realistically, a superintendent cannot hope to develop the perfect leadership profile, but it is essential to know what one can be.

NOTES

1. Carl Sandburg, *Abraham Lincoln: The War Years* (New York: Dell, 1925.) 732–33.

2. Edward Lewis and Jack Belck, *The Living Words of Abraham Lincoln* (Hallmark Cards, 1967), 17.

3. Lewis and Belck, *The Living Words of Abraham Lincoln,*14.

4. Lewis and Belck, *The Living Words of Abraham Lincoln,* 14.

5. David Donald, *Lincoln Reconsidered.* (New York: Vintage, 1961), 68.

6. *Abe Lincoln's Jokes, Wit and Humor* (Chicago: Stein, 1943). 58.

CHAPTER SEVENTEEN

Is the Superintendency the Right Job for You?

Especially after reading the previous chapter on leadership, some readers who might be considering becoming superintendents may have become less confident about their ability to be a success in the position. It is important to realize that there are no perfect leaders—and this includes Abraham Lincoln, as well as everyone who has served as a superintendent of schools. The purpose of this book is not to attempt to develop a generation of superintendents who will not make mistakes. Any chief school officer will make his or her share of errors, including lack of foresight, hiring less than competent people, and many other failures of judgment. There will also be times when any superintendent will not enjoy the job.

On the other hand, the superintendency can provide a career that allows for many wonderful experiences with children, faculty, staff, parents, and community members. Opportunities will abound for fellowship with other administrators and superintendents. Most often, superintendents have the respect of their community, and many people will greatly appreciate the kind words and help that a chief school officer can give. Superintendents also enjoy the opportunity to act as a mentor to future administrators and help prepare them as leaders.

In addition, the compensation as the chief executive in a school district is most often quite good. With the likely shortage of qualified candidates, salary and fringe benefits will probably only increase. The possibility of seeing programs that were initiated under your leadership actually improving teaching and learning in your district will also offer a great sense of satisfaction. Finally, superintendents can enjoy meeting with graduates of their school systems who are making a contribution in their communities and know that what they are doing was aided by the education they were given in the school district.

The next decade will be an excellent time to seek a position as a superintendent. The need and the demand for qualified candidates have never been greater. Education is currently a major priority of political leaders at both the national and state levels. This emphasis should ensure that adequate funding will be made available to improve programs in most school districts. The current posture of teacher unions is also encouraging. More than ever, they are talking about working cooperatively to raise the standards of the teaching profession. In addition, the teaching profession seems committed to ongoing staff development. There is also a positive trend toward additional parent and community involvement in schools. Finally, the potential impact of technology in our schools provides another opportunity for school leaders to bring about positive change.

As you consider whether the superintendency is an appropriate career goal, reflect on the following questions:

1. What is your motivation for seeking the position? Undoubtedly, a number of factors are causing you to consider becoming a superintendent. One major factor should be that you have a desire to help children. Money, respect, and prestige are not sufficient reasons to seek work in administration. Also, merely seeking to get out of the classroom is not the best motive. Certainly, a person's motivation will be a mixture of personal aspirations and professional goals, but not all of the motivation should be self-serving.

2. Do you like being in a public position? Specifically, are you prepared to speak before small and large groups and to spend a considerable amount of your day in meetings? Do you have effective communication skills, especially with other adults?

3. Have you developed a vision for the type of school system you would like to help create?

4. Can you deal with stressful situations such as debating issues and answering difficult questions in a public setting? Will you be able to dismiss an ineffective employee?

5. Can you sleep at night when you are facing complicated and unresolved dilemmas?

6. Can you function when you are dealing with a number of problems at the same time?

7. Is it possible for you to accept compromise and to live with ambiguity?

8. Can you make a decision and not cause yourself anguish by constantly second-guessing yourself?

9. Do you have the humility to admit mistakes and to take the heat when things are going wrong?

These are difficult questions, and it is impossible for someone to answer all of them truthfully if he or she has not yet experienced the pressures of administration. It is rather like combat in that people never know how they will react until they are in the situation. Still, most adults know themselves well enough to have some idea about the answers to some of these questions. Sometimes it is helpful to ask those who know you best to assess your ability to deal with the difficult aspects of administration.

If you feel that the superintendency is not an appropriate aspiration, this self-knowledge is also important. Too many superb teachers have left the classroom for administration and have lived to regret it.

One final admonition is in order. Do not become an administrator just because some people say you would be good at it. Although this type of positive encouragement is always flattering, *you* must feel some sense of calling. In many ways, it is a decision of the heart as well as the head. Even with the strong motivation to help bring about positive change, individuals must enter school administration with their eyes wide open. A superintendent especially cannot afford to be naïve about the inevitable pressures of the position. Your powers will be less absolute than you anticipate, and you will need to rely on other people to make a difference.

Most important, for those who do become superintendents, the potential for doing good provides an opportunity for true success. Because a superintendent has a prominent and visible position in the community, it provides an excellent opportunity for modeling an effective and productive life. One of the best descriptions of such a life is portrayed in this short poem by Ralph Waldo Emerson:

To laugh often and much;
to win the respect of intelligent people and the affection of children;
to earn the appreciation of honest critics and endure the betrayal of false friends;
to appreciate beauty;
to find the best in others;
to leave the world a bit better, whether by a healthy child, a garden patch or a redeemed social condition;
to know that even one life has breathed easier because you have lived.
This is to have succeeded.[1]

NOTES

1. *Great Quotations, 2000*, http://www.cybernation.com/vict.../quotes_emerson_ralph waldo.Htm> (12 June 2000).

INDEX

About the Author

Bill Hayes has been a high school social studies teacher, department chairman, assistant principal, and high school principal. From 1973 to 1994, he served as superintendent of schools for the Byron-Bergen Central School District, which is located eighteen miles west of Rochester, New York. During his career, he was an active member of the New York State Council of School Superintendents and is the author of a council publication entitled *The Superintendency: Thoughts for New Superintendents*, which is used to prepare new superintendents in New York state. Mr. Hayes has also written a number of articles for various educational journals. Since his retirement in 1994, he has chaired the Teacher Education Division at Roberts Wesleyan College in Rochester, New York. He is the author of *Real Life Case Studies for Teachers* and *Real Life Case Studies for Administrators*, which were published by Scarecrow Press in 2000.